# FIRE ESCAPE

## HOW ANIMALS AND PLANTS SURVIVE WILDFIRES

by **Jessica Stremer**

illustrated by
**Michael Garland**

books for a
better
earth

™
holiday house • new york

## A **Books for a Better Earth**™ Title

The Books for a Better Earth™ collection is designed to inspire young people to become active, knowledgeable participants in caring for the planet they live on. Focusing on solutions to climate change challenges and human environmental impacts, the collection looks at how scientists, activists, and young leaders are working to safeguard Earth's future.

Library of Congress Cataloging-in-Publication Data

Names: Stremer, Jessica, author. | Garland, Michael, 1952- illustrator.
Title: Fire escape : how animals and plants survive wildfires / by Jessica Stremer ; illustrated by Michael Garland.
Description: First edition. | New York : Holiday House, [2025] | Series: Books for a better earth | Includes bibliographical references and index. | Audience: Ages 8-12 | Audience: Grades 4-6 | Summary: "A timely middle grade book exploring the incredible ways animals detect, respond, and adapt to wildfires, as well as how climate change is affecting the frequency and severity of these devastating events in nature"– Provided by publisher.
Identifiers: LCCN 2023034535 | ISBN 9780823454426 (hardcover)
Subjects: LCSH: Animals–Effect of fires on. | Fire ecology. | Wildfires–Climatic factors.
Classification: LCC QH545.F5 S77 2024 | DDC 577.2/4–dc23/eng/20231208
LC record available at https://lccn.loc.gov/2023034535

ISBN: 978-0-8234-5442-6 (hardcover)

*To Mom, for showing me how to open doors*
*—J. S.*

*To my sister, Kathleen*
*—M. G.*

# TABLE OF CONTENTS

Night operations on the Pine Gulch Fire in Colorado

# WORLD ON FIRE

*Somewhere in the world, there's a wildfire burning.*

You've probably seen wildfires on the news, or maybe even experienced one where you live. Fires can be scary, but they're a natural part of the landscape. A wildfire, also called a forest fire, bushfire, or wildland fire, is an unplanned and potentially uncontrollable fire that burns through a vegetative area. Wildfires create ripples of changes to the ecosystem. The significance of those changes depends on the location and severity of the fire, as well as the plants and animals that live nearby.

Wildfires fall into three categories. **Ground fires** burn **organic** material, like tree roots and **peat**, which is buried below ground. They spread slowly, but they are more difficult to **extinguish** because firefighters can't see where or exactly how far underground a fire has spread.

**Surface fires** burn on the surface of the ground, consuming **fuel** such as grass, leaves, twigs, and shrubs. How fast a surface fire spreads depends on the amount of fuel and wind present during a fire and the shape of the landscape.

**Crown fires** burn leaves and branches at the top of a forest. They burn faster than surface fires because the top of a forest, also called the **canopy**, is exposed to more wind.

Ground and surface fires can spread to treetops by climbing the **fuel ladder**. A fuel ladder isn't something you'd use to climb things, but rather low-lying tree branches, shrubs, and smaller trees found under the canopy of a larger tree. With a little wind, flames can spread from this lower vegetation to treetops.

Have you ever wondered what happens to animals and plants during a wildfire, or how an ecosystem rebuilds after the flames go out? Are you curious about the tools and techniques firefighters use to battle the blaze, or interested to learn how an increase in megafires is changing everything? Let's turn up the heat and turn the page!

A wildfire burns at Ocala National Forest.

# JUST ONE SPARK

*Bzzz. Bzzz. Bzzz.*

You grab your phone, swipe open the home screen, and tap the icon:

"ALERT! Wildfire warning. Expect strong winds and warm, dry air. Fires will spread quickly. Be prepared!"

Somewhere nearby, a hot spark has landed in a pile of dry grass and leaves. Maybe the spark happened when a vehicle briefly scraped the pavement. Perhaps it was from a flash of lightning or a stray ember from a campfire. No matter where it came from, that tiny spark is about to cause big problems.

Heat reacts with oxygen in the air and fuel from the forest floor.

A fire burns along the ground in the Bitterroot National Forest.

In seconds, a wildfire is born.

*Bzzz. Bzzz. Bzzz.*

This time the alert reads:

"Wildfire spotted. EVACUATE NOW."

Humans use technology to stay in touch with the world around them. But animals don't have phones within paw's reach. So how do they know about a threat like a wildfire?

**Fire Fact!** Human-created hazards, such as unattended campfires, cigarettes tossed out of car windows, and fallen power lines, are responsible for nearly 90 percent of wildfires in the United States.

**Fire Fact!** It only takes one hot ember to ignite and destroy tens of thousands of acres of land.

**Fire Fact!** The National Weather Service issues red flag warnings to alert the public of conditions that may lead to the rapid spread of wildfires, including the combination of warm temperatures, low humidity, and strong winds.

## SENSING DANGER

Animals rely on their senses—smell, sound, and sight—to monitor their surroundings.

Smells, or **olfactory cues**, are often the first indication to wildlife that something isn't right. Have you ever smelled someone cooking on their grill from a few houses away? Just like people, animals often smell the smoke from a fire before they can see it.

Other **mammals** smell the same way people do. As they inhale, teeny-tiny odor particles floating through the air land on sensory receptors inside their noses. Those receptors send a message to the brain, which tells the animal what it's smelling. **Amphibians** and **reptiles** smell through something on the roof of their mouth called the **Jacobson's organ**. Insects detect odor particles in the air using smell-gathering organs located on their antennae.

No matter how an animal smells, they can all detect smoke. And where there's smoke, there's fire!

For some animals, their ability to detect sound is even better than their sense of smell. As your phone buzzes loud evacuation warnings, animals are hearing something entirely different—the forest burning.

The sound of a fire doesn't come from the flames. Instead, it comes from chemical reactions happening inside plants as they burn. Water and sap that are trapped within pockets of woody tissue of the plant heat up and transform into steam. As more steam is produced, it expands, pressing harder and harder on the inside of the plant until—*pop!*—the pockets burst open, and the steam escapes.

When a fire begins, these sounds may be soft. Think of leaves crackling in a firepit. But as a fire grows, consuming more and more fuel, that faint crackling becomes a roar. Firefighters have reported that extremely large fires sound like a freight train barreling through the forest.

If animals smell or hear something, they look for additional signs of danger. They may spot a stream of smoke rising from the landscape or notice if the usually blue sky now glows an eerie red. Some animals don't see color the way humans do, but they can detect if smoke is shadowing the sun or if flames are illuminating the usually dark night.

Fire Fact! Fire acts like a living organism. As plant material burns, hot air is created and smoke rises. Air from the ground is then pulled in, which creates wind. The wind helps push a fire forward, consuming even more plant material. The cycle continues. The wind gains speed, causing a fire to grow even larger and spread even faster.

Fire Fact! Fires will continue to burn unless one of the three fire ingredients—oxygen, fuel, or heat—is removed.

Fire Fact! Wildfires can reach up to 800°C (1,472°F) or more. That's hotter than a kitchen oven, which typically maxes out \at 500°C (932°F), but not as hot as the sun, whose inner \temperature can reach up to 15,000,000°C (27,000,000°F).

*Bzzz. Bzzz. Bzzz.*

"Tree on fire blocking Highway 9. Use a different route."

You pull up the map and check for updates on where the fire is burning and how fast it's spreading. Your phone may even suggest a route to the nearest place to take shelter. Luckily, animals don't have to stick to paved pathways to escape. But how do they decide where to go?

Most **birds** that detect fire simply fly away. Migratory birds passing through the area will keep flying, avoiding the smoky skies as much as possible. For animals without wings, lifting off to a fire-free area isn't an option. Once again, they rely on their senses to determine where a fire is located and where it's headed.

Winds can carry smoke odor molecules hundreds of miles away. If animals begin traveling in one direction and the smell grows stronger, they'll turn around and try a different path. If the popping, crackling, and sizzling sounds of burning plants grow louder, animals instinctively know they need to go another way.

A hawk soars over the 416 Fire near Durango, Colorado.

Just as you know the buildings and roads near your home, animals also memorize their surroundings. Animals take note of familiar landmarks such as a pile of rocks, a large tree, or a stream. Using these landmarks and their senses to guide them, animals travel *away* from a fire and *toward* safety. They look for areas of refuge such as waterways, open fields, rocky patches, or ground that has already burned.

But survival requires knowing more than which way to go. The physical features of the land also play a part in how easily wildlife flees from fires.

Animals living in the middle of a dense forest might have a hard time escaping as toppling trees block their path and thick smoke makes it difficult to see and breathe. On the other hand, the exit route for animals living near a farm field may be wide open.

Some mammals join frogs and other amphibians in nearby ponds and lakes. During a surface fire, animals with the ability to climb, such as raccoons, may choose to scurry up a tree and out of the fire's reach.

When you can't fly, can't run, and can't climb or swim, there's only one option left.

Hide.

Beneath the forest floor lie holes, burrows, and tunnels. Many of these underground hideaways have multiple entrances that supply animals with fresh air and an emergency exit. Rodents squeeze under stumps. Snakes slither under rocks. Even insects retreat underground, where just a few inches of soil offer protection from the heat and flames raging overhead.

But even then, survival is not guaranteed.

Fire Fact! Different species of animals have been found sharing the same burrow during a wildfire.

Fire Fact! A tree's outer layer of bark acts as a shield against the flames for animals and insects hiding underneath or inside the tree. Even a dead tree can be a safe place to hide, depending on the type of fire.

Fire Fact! Many large mammals, such as deer and bears, will circle back to areas that have recently burned to wait out a fire.

# LIVESTOCK ON THE LOOSE

*A wildfire is heading straight for your house.*

Before hopping in your car to evacuate, you toss your phone, a charger, and a few other things in a bag. You coax your dog out from under the bed. But your cat has disappeared somewhere inside the house, and your pet lizard is down in the basement. Time is running out. Your parents tell you to forget them and get in the car. Now!

Sadly, many people are forced to leave their pets behind during a wildfire. And for farms and ranches with hundreds of animals, evacuating animals is even harder.

Like their wild counterparts, horses, sheep, cattle, and other livestock can smell and hear an approaching wildfire. If a fire is burning far away, livestock probably won't change their behavior. But as a fire moves closer, livestock often become more vocal, warning others with louder neighs, baas, and moos that something is wrong.

Unlike wild animals, livestock are stuck behind fences and trapped inside their pens. As they grow more agitated, animals may pace back and forth or paw at the gates of their stalls trying to open them. Groups of animals in the same pen may huddle together, watching, waiting.

Helpless.

To avoid this, most farms prepare for wildfires. When phones buzz with an evacuation warning, everyone living and working on the farm knows just what to do.

Owners place smaller animals in crates and carriers, which are then stacked in the back of vehicles. Larger animals are loaded onto special transport trailers. If there's time, owners may also grab food, medicine, and other supplies for the animals before friends and neighbors arrive to help haul the animals away.

**Fire Fact!** Local county animal response teams, called CARTs for short, may be called in to help with the evacuation if the owner doesn't have enough trucks and trailers to transport their animals. CARTs are made up of volunteers who prepare and train for animal evacuations during wildfire emergencies.

Sometimes evacuations don't go as planned. Smoke chokes the air, making it difficult for both people and animals to see and breathe. Temperatures rise. Panic sets in.

Animals can sense when people are afraid, and their reactions make rescue more challenging. Smaller animals may hide or run in circles. Larger animals trained to board trailers, such as horses, may refuse to be led on. Frightened and stressed by a change in their routine, animals might break free from their owner.

Training an animal to board a trailer may make evacuating during a wildfire emergency easier.

The more an animal resists, the more dangerous the evacuation becomes. Animals could run into burning barns or injure themselves on tools and equipment. While moving a panicking animal, owners could get knocked over and trampled.

It's a race against the clock to get animals and their owners safely away from the deadly flames.

Fire Fact! People use a variety of methods to tag their animals depending on the type of animal and the size of the herd. Spray paint in various colors or patterns may be sprayed on the animal's side. Permanent marker is used to write on an animal's hoof. Metal or plastic tags, similar to earrings people wear, may be attached to an animal's ear. Special tags are quickly clipped into a horse's mane. If an animal is found wandering after a fire has stopped burning, these tags tell volunteers who the animal belongs to.

Have you ever practiced a safety drill at school? Sometimes the drill requires you to leave the building. Other times you need to find a safe spot within the building, also known as **sheltering in place**.

If a fire is advancing too quickly or there are too many animals to transport, evacuating may not be an option. In that case, farmers try to protect their animals by sheltering them in place, moving the animals into structures such as barns and stables. This can cause problems if there aren't enough stalls to safely separate the animals, who may act aggressively towards one another and even get injured as they all cram together.

This special tag can be quickly clipped to a horse's mane during a wildfire emergency.

Another danger of sheltering in place is the risk of the structure catching fire. To prevent this, owners may spray water on the roof and exterior walls.

There's also the chance that smoke could blow inside through vents and cracks in the siding and doors, making it difficult for animals to breathe.

With every passing moment, stress and fear builds.

What about large groups of livestock that won't fit inside buildings? Ranchers who need to evacuate thousands of cattle or sheep face these same challenges—and more. If there's time, they might shelter them in place by herding animals to a safer location. Perhaps next to a pond or stream or a freshly plowed field which contains less flammable material.

Eventually time runs out. Animal owners must make the difficult decision to stay and fight a fire, risking their own lives, or leave their animals behind.

Owners often open pens, stalls, and gates to give animals an opportunity to flee. They'll turn off the power to electric fences, decreasing the chance of injury if an animal gets pushed against the fence by others in the herd. Owners will also turn sprinklers on to keep the ground wet, in hopes of preventing buildings and fields from catching fire. If there's

time, owners may set out extra food and water for the animals to eat and drink until—or if—they are able to return.

Livestock, now on the loose, must rely on its **instincts** to survive.

> Fire Fact! Burning forests and fields aren't the only threat to animals during a wildfire. A fallen power line that still has electricity flowing to it can electrocute any living thing that touches it. Propane tanks full of flammable gas can explode. Burning embers can land on hay bales, causing them to catch fire. Farmers try to steer clear of these hazards when relocating their animals.
>
> Fire Fact! Firefighters always work to save the lives of people first. They try to help pets and livestock if possible. Saving buildings is a firefighter's lowest priority.

## ZOOS

Farms and ranches aren't the only places where large numbers of animals rely on people for care. Zoos are home to thousands of rare and exotic birds, reptiles, amphibians, and mammals. Just like farms, zoos have emergency plans in place to ensure the safety of visitors, staff, and animals. Zoos also plan to protect supplies and equipment needed to care for these special animals. Preparation is key to survival.

Zoo animals are trained to work with humans. They are accustomed to tasks such as standing still during a nail trimming, cooperating during health checkups, and relocating to a different enclosure. They get rewarded with food every time they do what the zookeeper asks. This reward reinforces and encourages the desired behavior. Zookeepers rely on this training during a wildfire emergency.

When the threat of wildfire is especially high, such as on hot, dry, windy days, or when a wildfire is already burning nearby, zookeepers may remove transport crates from storage and set them near each animal's exhibit. They monitor weather conditions closely so that, when the time comes, they can jump into action.

Relocating zoo animals comes with unique sets of challenges. Certain dangerous mammals, such as lions, may be **tranquilized** in order for zookeepers to safely handle them. Some animals are simply too large to evacuate during an emergency. Elephants, for example, need extra-large crates and heavy-duty trucks to transport them. Giraffes are too tall to fit under freeway overpasses. Don't worry, zookeepers have a plan for them too!

These animals shelter in place, moving to areas of the zoo that firefighters can more easily defend against the flames. Even the zoo parking lot may become a holding area for animals sheltering on-site.

As the wildfire advances, zookeepers communicate with first responders to let them know where the animals are being kept. They also let them know if there are any animals, such as those that are endangered, that may need more protection than others.

Zoos use **generators** to supply power to buildings where animals shelter. Unlike structures on farms, which may be susceptible to heat and smoke, many zoo buildings have air filtration systems to provide clean air for animals and air-conditioning to keep them comfortable.

Just like on farms, sprinklers go off throughout the zoo to keep the ground wet and to help prevent a fire from spreading. Zookeepers fill trash cans, buckets, and other containers with extra water in case the water supply is cut off or contaminated with ash and debris.

Zookeepers often risk their own lives by staying at the zoo to care for the animals. They may join in the fight, using fire extinguishers and hoses to put out small fires that start inside the zoo while firefighters fight the flames around the zoo's perimeter. They also watch the animals closely for signs of stress, breathing issues, or injuries.

Whether it's a zoo housing thousands of animals, a ranch with hundreds of cattle, or a small farm, having a plan for wildfire is a must. Preparation, practice, and working together are key to both the animals' and their caretakers' survival.

Fire Fact! Nearby zoos and aquariums often work together during an emergency by loaning supplies to each other. Sometimes animals are relocated to another facility when the threat of fire is high, even if one isn't burning yet.

Fire Fact! Open areas like parking lots act as a firebreak, a strip of unburnable land that helps stop the spread of fire. They also allow fresh air to circulate.

Fire Fact! While all animals are important, some receive priority care over other animals in the zoo. This includes animals that are considered highly endangered, animals that are valuable for breeding, and "ambassador animals" that people visit the zoo to see most frequently.

# SURROUNDED BY DANGER

Content warning: This chapter discusses sensitive topics including animal injury and death.

*One spark.* One tiny flame can grow into a massive fire in only minutes. While many animals are able to flee wildfire, not all of them make it out unharmed.

Pets who hide or run away during an evacuation may find themselves trapped inside a burning building. Livestock who are cut loose or break free from their owners often retreat back to their stalls, becoming trapped when flames block their exit. For wild animals living near a fire's origin, there may simply not be enough time to get away.

Animals that do flee may inadvertently fall victim to firefighting activity. Sometimes animals are spooked by low-flying aircraft dropping water or **fire-retardant chemicals**. Others may encounter firefighters operating bulldozers, chain saws, or other machinery. The noise scares and confuses the animals.

These creatures face a choice:

- Continue away from fire and toward people, whom they instinctively fear, or
- Double back toward the fire and try to find another escape route.

As a fire grows in size and strength, fleeing becomes more difficult. Burning branches, leaves, and twigs falling from the forest canopy can injure animals. Toxic chemicals in smoke cause lungs

to burn and eyes to sting. Extreme heat singes hair and skin and causes painful blisters. The ground, as hot as coals from a campfire, sears the pads of animals' feet as they move across the scorched landscape one painful step at a time.

Some animals have lower odds for surviving a wildfire. Birds that build nests on the ground, such as wild turkeys, can't easily fly away from a fire. If a fire starts at night, birds roosting on lower branches of trees may not even have time to react. Adult birds often suffer from smoke inhalation as they circle back through a fire to check on their chicks.

Animals such as raccoons, squirrels, baby birds that do not yet have the ability to fly, or animals who have climbed up a tree to avoid fire on the ground may find themselves trapped if a fire spreads to the crown of the tree. Snakes in the middle of shedding their skin can't easily slide under a rock or stump for protection. Young, old, sick, and injured animals who are unable to see and move well are often left behind as other animals flee.

Even after a wildfire passes, animals remain in danger. Birds may be electrocuted if they land on damaged power lines. Other animals are picked off by predators who take advantage of the open landscape, leaving fewer places for **prey** to hide. Many animals, after spending hours avoiding the flames, are too thirsty, tired, or injured to continue on.

While the exact number of animals that die during wildfires each year is unknown, scientists believe many more survive and overcome their injuries. Some even receive help from people. But first, rescuers have to find them.

Fire Fact! Smoke is made up of a mixture of fine particles and gases. Wildfire smoke contains carbon monoxide, a colorless, odorless, and toxic gas that causes headaches, dizziness, and nausea. Carbon monoxide also decreases a person's or animal's ability to think clearly.

Fire Fact! Flames can appear different colors depending on what type of material is being consumed and how hot a fire is burning. Sodium—which you might know is found in table salt—is also found in most kinds of wood. Sodium burns orange or dark yellow. Carbon and hydrogen create a blue flame, while copper creates green or blue flames.

Fire Fact! Embers from still-burning logs, stumps, and piles of leaf litter remain burning even after fire in the surrounding area has been extinguished. These hot spots can spread or flare up when strong gusts of wind blow through the area.

## SEARCH AND RESCUE

When people return to their homes and farms, surviving pets and livestock are rescued from the rubble and taken to veterinarians for care. But for animals living deep in the forest, rescue may not come for days or weeks.

Thanks to recently formed groups like the **Wildlife Disaster Network (WDN)**, animals have a better chance at being rescued than ever before. Pilots sometimes spot and report the location of an injured animal as they fly over a burned area to survey the damage.

Other times, firefighters discover injured animals hiding beneath still-smoldering rubble or clinging to life at the top of a tree.

When firefighters say it's safe, WDN trained volunteers slog through the ash, climb steep hillsides, step over charred logs, and wade through streams searching for animals in need of help. These searches can last days or even months depending on the acres burned and the number of volunteers.

Fire Fact! In 2020, Dr. Jamie Peyton flew to Australia to treat animals injured during devastating bushfires. She noticed that volunteers—including veterinarians, wildlife biologists, and ecologists—teamed up with firefighters and rescue workers to search for and save wild animals. Inspired by their efforts, Dr. Peyton founded the United States Wildlife Disaster Network (WDN), which locates and rescues animals injured from wildfires in the United States. Members of the WDN work alongside Veterinarian Emergency Response Teams (VERTs) to quickly and efficiently mobilize the resources needed to help animals affected by wildfire and other disasters.

Fire Fact! Many wild animals are unable to get enough food and water following a wildfire. People may want to help, but offering too much water or the wrong type of food may do more harm than good. If you discover a hurt animal, do not approach it. Ask a local animal rescue organization or veterinarian for help.

## INITIAL CARE

Rescued wild animals are taken to treatment facilities. Care teams record data about each animal, including where the animal was found, its size and weight, and a full list of its injuries. X-rays identify broken or fractured bones. An ultrasound reveals any injuries to its internal organs. A blood sample shows electrolyte imbalances and how the liver, kidney, and pancreas are functioning.

Red and white blood cell counts tell the veterinarian if the animal has an infection. Putting this information together helps the care team decide what kind of treatment the animal needs.

The first thing a care team focuses on is getting the animal **hydrated**. They may offer water for the animal to drink or give it fluids through an **intravenous (IV)** tube just as doctors do for humans in the hospital. Care teams also give antibiotics to treat infections and pain medicine for the animal to feel more comfortable.

A few days of fluids, food, rest, and medicine may be enough to release animals with minor injuries back into the wild. Those with more severe injuries may take weeks or months to recover.

Unfortunately, some animals' injuries are too severe. When this happens, a care team may make the difficult decision to **euthanize** the animal rather than extend its suffering.

---

**Fire Fact!** Burns to the skin are broken down into four categories:

- First-degree burns affect the outer layer of the skin, called the epidermis. A mild sunburn is an example of a first-degree burn.

- Second-degree burns affect the first and second layer of the skin, called the dermis. The burn site may be red, swollen, and blistered.

- Third-degree burns destroy the first and second layers of the skin and damage underlying tissue.

- Fourth-degree burns go beyond the skin, injuring layers of fat, muscle, and bone.

The more severe the burn, the greater the treatment required for the skin to heal.

The type of care animals receive after being stabilized depends on the species of animal and the animal's specific injuries.

Mammals are the most common class of animal rescued. Many suffer severe burns to their skin, ears, and eyes, though they can usually recover from injuries to these parts of the body without medical care. However, burns on the pads of their feet are a different story.

Have you ever had a blister on the back of your heel? It hurts to walk. Now imagine your entire foot being covered in blisters. Animals with burns on the bottom of their feet have a hard time moving and finding food. If left untreated, those injuries become a death sentence.

Let's look at the case of a bobcat that wound up in the care of a team from the Gold Country Wildlife Rescue Center in Auburn, California. During the initial evaluation, the team discovered the bottoms of the bobcat's feet were burned through to the bone. The bobcat was **emaciated** from lack of food and **dehydrated** from lack of water.

The care team could tell the bobcat was in an enormous amount of pain, yet he lashed out as they tried to help him. This behavior was a good sign. It meant the bobcat had a strong will to live and a healthy fear of people. The team needed to act quickly. If the bobcat didn't receive help soon, he would die.

Thankfully, a new treatment offered hope for the animal.

In 2017, Dr. Jamie Peyton, a veterinarian at the University of California, Davis **pioneered** a treatment for burns that uses the body part of another animal—the skin of a tilapia fish.

A bobcat receives care for burns that occurred during a wildfire.

Tilapia is commonly farmed for people to eat, and their skins are usually discarded. Dr. Peyton identified several traits that make the skin uniquely helpful when repurposed as a burn treatment for animals: it is cheaper, more abundant, and easier to obtain than traditional burn treatment supplies, like **gauze**. Tilapia skin is very flexible, making it easy to use on a variety of differently shaped burn areas such as faces, legs, and pads of feet. Most importantly, tilapia skin contains high amounts of a healing protein called **collagen**. Collagen provides natural pain relief and greatly speeds up recovery time.

Before it can be used, the tilapia skin is **sanitized** to remove blood, germs, and fishy odor. The care team **sedates** the wounded animal, then begins treatment. It cleans damaged tissue with soap and cool water and cuts off any loose skin. Next, the tilapia skin is placed, flesh side down, directly on the injured tissue. The surgeon then stitches the fish skin into the healthy skin of the mammal. Finally, the area is wrapped in corn husks, rice paper (for adult bears and mountain lions), or cotton padding and gauze (for smaller mammals) to add a layer of protection between the burn site and the ground and to delay the animal from chewing off the tilapia bandage.

Left: Dr. Jamie Peyton fits a biologic bandage made of tilapia skin over the burned pads of a mountain lion cub.
Right: Dr. Jamie Peyton applies a bandage made of tilapia skin to second-degree burns on a dog.

If you think the idea of using fish skin as a Band-Aid sounds gross, you're probably not alone. But wild animals aren't bothered by it. They want to be released back into the wild. The sooner, the better, to avoid becoming dependent on humans. And in the case of the bobcat at the Gold Country Wildlife Rescue Center, this strategy worked out.

Shortly after waking up from surgery, the bobcat was back on his feet, pacing his enclosure. Just three days later, Dr. Peyton removed the tilapia skin bandage to discover new tissue was already growing over the bone. Eleven weeks after treatment, the bobcat was returned to the wild. In all likelihood, he would have died if not for this lifesaving treatment.

Fire Fact! Many animals eat fish. Removing the fishy smell usually allows the tilapia bandage to remain on for a longer period of time.

Injured pads aren't the only body part that causes mammals trouble. Mammals use claws to grasp prey and climb trees. Some mammals, such as bobcats, have claws that retract or partially retract into their paws, which protects them from injury. But some don't, which is how a pair of gray foxes ended up at the Gold Country Wildlife Rescue Center.

Both foxes had significant injuries to their claws, something only time could heal. Unfortunately, time was not on their side. Without the ability to climb and hunt for food, the foxes' chance of survival was low. The team cared for the foxes for five months as it waited for the foxes' claws to regrow. Before releasing the foxes, the scientists tested the strength of the foxes' new claws by placing food high up in a tree and ensuring the pair could successfully climb to reach it.

Birds are less commonly rescued. When they are, their recovery can take even longer. Injuries from smoke inhalation are treated with inhalers and nebulizers, but the biggest concern for birds is damage to their wings. They need the ability to fly and hunt to survive.

To speed up the recovery and release process, some birds, especially birds of prey such as raptors, may have their feathers fixed through a process called imping. **Imping** involves taking a **molted** feather from a different bird, usually of the same species, and joining it to the damaged feather of the injured bird. A thin piece of bamboo, metal wire, or other material is used to connect the shafts of the two feathers together. A bit of glue applied to the connection site ensures the new feather stays in place.

Burney the owl suffered damage to his wings from a wildfire.

Burney the owl, fully recovered on the night of his release back into the wild

Birds with imped wings can be released back into the wild in a matter of weeks. When the bird eventually molts, the imped feathers will fall out and be replaced with new ones. However, if too many feathers are damaged on a rescued bird, imping isn't an option. The care team must wait for the bird to go through at least one molt before releasing it.

Reptiles and amphibians are not typically recovered after a wildfire because they are smaller and tend to hide from people. An injured snake or turtle is much more difficult to spot than a bear or bobcat. If reptiles or amphibians are found, care teams provide treatment to meet their individual needs.

## RETURN TO THE WILD

It's important that rescued animals do not become dependent on humans; they need to be able to find food for themselves when they return to their natural habitats. To help wild animals stay wild, care teams interact with them as little as possible. They often wear masks to prevent animals from seeing their faces and keep conversation minimal around the enclosures.

Feeding the animals is the trickiest to navigate. Care teams often place live prey inside an animal's enclosure. At first the prey may be completely immobilized so that it's easier for the animals to catch. As animals heal, care teams encourage them to hunt by offering prey that can move around inside the enclosure.

A series of photos showing the process for imping the feathers of a great horned owl

But how do care teams know when an animal is ready to be released back into the wild if they avoid interacting with it? Cameras inside the enclosure allow a care team to watch the animal's behavior and monitor its progress. They watch for signs the animal is ready to be released, such as regaining full use of its body and successful hunting. They also watch to make sure the animal demonstrates a fear of people whenever the care team is around.

Choosing where to release a rehabilitated animal is an important decision. Care teams look for a spot somewhat close to where the animal was found, but that's not always possible if the fire destroyed too much of the animal's resources. Teams prioritize areas that offer plenty of food, water, and shelter and, if possible, are far away from people. They might also confer with local scientists to make sure the new home is appropriate.

While a recently burned area may not have enough food or shelter available to support the rescued animal, other animals can survive—and even thrive—in the postfire landscape.

Fire Fact! Some animals are simply too young, require too much hands-on care, or rely too much on people for survival to be released back into the wild. Instead, they are rehomed at zoos and wildlife centers.

Fire Fact! Collars or other tracking devices are sometimes placed on rescued animals, allowing scientists to monitor their movement after being released. Knowing where an animal has traveled after release can help scientists decide where to release other animals in the future.

Fire Fact! Seasonal weather conditions also play a role in when an animal is released back into the wild.

# CHAPTER 4

# SIZZLING OPPORTUNITIES

*Not all animals flee fire.* Some use it to their advantage.

During slow-burning surface fires, predators such as bears, coyotes, raccoons, and hawks hunt just ahead of the flames. In Australia, raptors nicknamed "fire hawks" have been observed picking up a burning stick with their talons, then dropping it to spread the fire. Scientists think they do this to aid with hunting.

Some animals depend on fire for the survival of their species. Fire-chasing beetles, also known as charcoal beetles, need trees damaged or killed by fire to reproduce. But where do these insects come from, and how do they find fire?

Charcoal beetles locate wildfires using tiny sensory pits located below their middle legs. Each pit, which looks similar to an insect eye, contains about seventy dome-shaped sensors. These sensors signal to the beetle that there's heat nearby.

Following these signals, the beetles swarm the area, sometimes even as a fire continues to burn. Heat and smoke protect the beetles from predators, allowing males and females to reproduce. Once the flames die down, females bore under the bark of burned trees and lay their eggs. For the well-protected beetle larvae, the inside of a burned tree provides a feast of nutrients. A year later, the larvae emerge from the tree as adults and fly away to take their chances in the world.

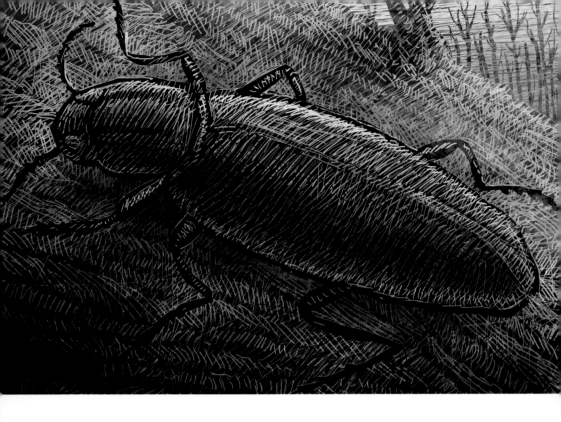

Charcoal beetles aren't the only winged wildlife that gravitates toward smoky skies. Horntail wasps, nicknamed "wood wasps," also use dead trees to sustain their larvae. Females insert a long egg-depositing organ called an **ovipositor** deep into the wood of trees damaged by fire, wind, and disease. Much like the charcoal beetle, the wasp larvae feed on the dead tree. Nearly two years later, the larva emerge from the tree as adult wasps.

A horntail wasp, also called a wood wasp

Fire Fact! Firefighters are sometimes bitten by charcoal beetles, who mistake the firefighter's warm body for a smoldering tree.

Fire Fact! Wood from fire-burned trees is sometimes harvested and turned into lumber. The lumber is then used for buildings. Wood wasp larvae may survive in the wood, even after harvesting. A few years later, people may be surprised to find wood wasps emerging from inside their homes!

Fire Fact! Snags are dead trees that are left upright to decompose naturally. When a snag (or part of a snag) falls on the ground, it becomes a log.

## A HELPING BEAK

This flurry of insect activity attracts hungry predators after the smoke has cleared. In many western U.S. forests, black-backed woodpeckers are first on the scene. For this species of bird, the seemingly unlivable habitat brims with opportunity. Mating insects provide a feast of nourishment while snags offer the perfect place for a new home. Black-backed woodpeckers use their hard, sharp beaks to drill a cavity into a tree. Inside the cavity, they create a nest. Soon there will be a clutch of newly hatched babies.

After a season of living in the snag, pieces of eggshell, old food, and poop clutter the woodpecker's cavity. The woodpecker family flies off in search of a new tree. But this pre-drilled home won't stay vacant for long.

**Secondary-cavity nesters**, including chickadees, bluebirds, and owls, are birds that use holes or cavities deserted by other cavity nesters. These birds' beaks aren't designed to drill into trees the way woodpeckers can. They depend on abandoned holes created by other animals for nests—sometimes even kicking other species out so they can use the space.

The postfire opportunities don't stop with insects and birds. As small mammals like chipmunks, squirrels, opossums, and raccoons return to the area, they also make homes and start families in abandoned woodpecker cavities. This growing population soon attracts larger predators back to the area.

A tree ring cross section depicts fire-scarring of a tree trunk, showing charred areas later encased in new growth. These scars are one method for dating fires in forest history.

While a wildfire is deadly for some, for many it means new life.

Fire Fact! Black-backed woodpeckers are sometimes used as an indicator species. The presence or absence of an indicator species can tell scientists how a habitat is changing and help guide efforts to manage the forest.

Fire Fact! The dark, charred color of a burnt tree helps the black-backed woodpecker blend into its surroundings.

Fire Fact! Researchers from the U.S. Forest Service Pacific Southwest Research Station (PSW) found that as many as 85 percent of woodpecker cavities were used by other animals in the first year after the cavity was created.

## CHAPTER 5

# EXPLODING PINE CONES

*A blackened forest might look like a graveyard for plants.* But looks can be deceiving! Just as animals have **adapted** to survive wildfires, plants also have a few tricks up their trunks.

## TRICK #1: LET IT GO

Eucalyptus trees, giant sequoia, certain types of pine, and many others have the potential to grow taller than flames from a ground or surface fire can reach. Still, height alone isn't always enough to prevent the canopy of a tree from catching fire. To protect their energy-making tops, some trees periodically drop unhealthy or lower branches through a process called **cladoptosis**.

A tree sheds a branch through the process of cladoptosis.

Cladoptosis is similar to **deciduous trees** shedding their leaves in the fall, except it can happen any time of the year. First, the tree stops sending food and water to the branch. Then, the tree seals off the branch's connection to the trunk. Eventually, the branch falls to the ground. Without lower branches, the tops of these tall trees remain unharmed during smaller fires.

## TRICK #2: COAT OF ARMOR

A tree's bark is its first line of defense against the outside world—including raging hot flames. The thick dead outer layer of bark acts like armor and protects the tree's living inner portion from damage.

Certain trees that grow in areas prone to wildfires, such as coast live oaks, have evolved to produce a thicker layer of bark, allowing them to better withstand hot flames. But thick bark and a tall crown don't always guarantee a tree's survival.

If a fire burns too hot for too long, the outer layer of bark is bound to suffer damage. Just below the outer bark lies a layer of dividing cells called **cambium tissue**, which generates new inner and outer bark. If the cambium tissue becomes damaged during a wildfire, no new growth occurs. And if that damage reaches the inner bark, the tree's ability to transport water and nutrients decreases. Add wood-boring insects into the mix, and the tree's chance of survival drops further.

But hope is not lost! Many trees have adapted yet another strategy to help the next generation survive.

A tree reproduces through seeds, which travel via wind, water, and animals to a new location where they will someday sprout and take root. Some seeds require an additional ingredient to **germinate**: fire!

For **pyrophilic seeds**, compounds in smoke act like an alarm clock, signaling to the seed that it's time to wake up.

Other pyrophilic seeds sprout because of changes to nutrients in the soil after a fire has passed. When a plant or animal dies, nutrients from its body (such as nitrogen, phosphorus, and sulfur) are recycled back into the ground, where they can be used by other living things. **Nutrient recycling** typically takes years, but fire speeds up the process. The seeds, roots, and buds that survived the fire gorge themselves on an influx of new energy from burned organic matter. Up from the ashes, new life sprouts.

For certain unusual plants, such as lodgepole pines, fire is the *only* trigger for germination. These plants have special seeds hidden inside **serotinous cones**. A glue-like substance called resin keeps the cones sealed shut, which protects their seeds from being eaten by predators.

Then, when a wildfire rips through the forest, the heat from the flames melts away the resin. The cones *explode* open. Seeds shoot through the air like popcorn kernels in a microwave! Some land at the base of the tree, while others get blown away to take root someplace else.

What about other plants, like bushes and grasses that lack the protection of thick bark or the ability to self-prune branches? This greenery has a different survival strategy hidden within its stems.

Fire Fact! A seed bank is the supply of seeds present in a given area. Some seeds are transient, meaning they have a limited amount of time to sprout before they die. Other seeds are persistent and can lie dormant for years before sprouting.

Fire Fact! Pyrophytes are plants that have adapted, or changed over time, in a way that makes them resistant to fire.

Fire Fact! Following an extensive fire, the canopy of a forest may be destroyed. That means newly dropped lodgepole pine seeds will have plenty of sunshine to soak up. With time, they'll grow tall and mighty, eventually producing serotinous cones of their own.

Have you ever noticed a new twig growing from an established branch, or a new plant emerging randomly out of the soil? Hidden and protected below ground or beneath layers of bark, new buds wait patiently for their turn to grow. A plant's actively growing branches and leaves produce a growth hormone that signals to these dormant buds, "We've got this! Sit back and relax." But when something destroys those leaves and branches, such as fire, the growth hormone disappears and the buds have a chance to sprout.

An epicormic shoot on a burned eucalyptus tree along the Great Alpine Road in Victoria, Australia. These shoots allow the tree to continue photosynthesizing while the tree canopy regrows.

Sprouting requires energy, though, and the leaves that plants use to make energy have just been burned up. So, what does a plant use to fuel its regrowth?

Just as people keep a stock-pile of food for an emergency, plants store extra energy and nutrients in their roots. After a fire, plants use these stored-up nutrients to produce new leaves. The new leaves begin harnessing the sun's energy to make more food and to re-plenish the emergency stash. This growth of new plant material is called **resprouting**.

Plants that have been grow-ing for a few seasons and have a well-developed root system with lots of stored energy may be able to resprout soon after a fire. This saved energy also allows established plants to grow faster than newly sprouted seeds. Newer plants might save their energy and resprout during the next grow-ing season.

For plants, there's no escaping a fire. Damage and injury are in-evitable. A plant's ability to make it through alive not only depends on its survival tactics, but also the age and health of the plant and the severity of the fire itself.

Dead plants continue to play an important role in supporting new life after the flames subside. All that charred wood is about to do a lot of good.

Fire Fact! Each fire burns differently depending on a combination of factors: the plants growing in an area, the health of these plants, the time of the year, and environmental factors such as recent rainfall. Imagine a lush, green forest. Now imagine a dry hillside that hasn't had rain for months. Which do you think would burn more easily?

# AFTER THE APOCALYPSE

*A wildfire can reduce a thriving forest* to nothing more than snags and ash, destroying animal homes and claiming many lives. Yet fire offers a chance to rebuild, since changes to the landscape introduce the possibility of new beginnings.

A bird makes a nest in a burned tree in Bryce Canyon National Park, Utah.

## ·················· SUCCESS WITH SUCCESSION ··················

The regrowth of the forest is called **succession,** and it happens in phases over hundreds of years. The first new plants on the scene after a fire are often weeds, which flower and produce new seeds quickly. Grasses may also join in on the growth. After a year or two, grasses and smaller shrubs often take over, and weeds can no longer grow.

Next come the **pioneer trees**. These trees are scrubby and slow-growing. They don't taste good to hungry animals—an evolutionary trick that helps ensure their survival over other plants. Alongside pioneer trees, sprouts from trees that survived the fire also grow during the first few years of succession. The surviving trees and pioneer trees eventually tower over the grasses and small plants. Their canopy blocks out the sun, slowing down the speed at which the smaller plants grow.

As the initial decades of growth pass, seeds from larger, more **hardy** species of trees get carried in by animals, or transported to the area by wind and water. These trees work their way up through the shrub canopy and begin to shade out shorter pioneer trees. Over the next sixty or more years, the area transforms from a young forest to a mature forest.

> Fire Fact! In some forests, trees can live to be well over a hundred years old. Undisturbed by people and unaltered through natural events, scientists call this an "old-growth" forest. Giant trees dominate the landscape, while smaller trees, shrubs, ferns, and moss grow beneath the older trees' thick canopy. Woody debris from dead or dying trees adds to the forest's diverse makeup.
>
> Fire Fact! The rate of regrowth and succession varies depending on the landscape, the types of plants growing in the area, and the severity of the fire.
>
> Fire Fact! Trees like alders, poplars, birches, and willows are all examples of pioneer species. They are often the first trees to grow in an area disturbed by fires, floods, or landslides.

## · · · · · · · · · · · · · · · · TORPOR TIME · · · · · · · · · · · · · · · ·

Survival in a postfire world is more of an uphill battle for animals.

Let's say a small rodent has just endured a wildfire. It crawls out of its hiding hole and discovers that the world looks drastically different from when it crawled in.

Should it:

A. Pack a bag of snacks and stay with friends?
B. Hang a "house wanted" sign and wait for help to come along?
C. Crawl back into its hiding hole and take a nap?

This decision is critical to survival. Surprisingly, for many small animals, option "C" is the best bet.

Doves, hummingbirds, mice, chipmunks, bats, and many other small mammals survive the postfire period by entering a state of **torpor**. During torpor, animals lower their body temperature and enter into a light, sleeplike state similar to hibernation. But unlike hibernating animals, who plan for a long period without food and water by building up a layer of fat, going into torpor following a fire is usually a sudden, lifesaving decision.

The animals stay in torpor anywhere from a few hours to a few days. While awake, they forage for food, drink water, and scout out the area to see if conditions have improved enough to become fully active. If not, they'll return to torpor and try again later.

In between periods of torpor, the animals may search for somewhere safer to make their new home. It could be a large pile of rocks, a group of trees still standing, or even a log brought down by the fire. In fact, that dead hunk of wood lying on the forest floor is an oasis to many small animals. Worms and ants living below the wood provide food, while the inside of the log provides protection from predators.

 **Fire Fact!** How often the forest burns, the time of year it typically burns, and the intensity of a fire make up a fire regime for a particular forest. Different regimes influence the types of plants and animals that live in an area as well as how quickly that area recovers after the fire goes out.

## MOVING ON

For other animals, there simply isn't enough food or protection nearby, and returning to the burned patch of forest they've just fled isn't an option. These animals travel until they reach someplace with shelter, food, and water. But traveling can expose an animal to hungry predators, so finding an unburned patch of forest quickly is critical to their survival.

When different parts of a forest burn at different times, they make up what scientists call a **patchwork** of burned and unburned areas. An easy way to understand a patchwork landscape is to picture the forest as a four-corner intersection. If all four corners of the intersection burn at once, the entire neighborhood must leave. Nearby neighborhoods don't have the right type of food or enough houses for displaced residents. The neighborhoods that have these resources are too far away—the chances of survival are slim.

A deer walks through a recently burned forest. The forest has already begun to regenerate.

On the other hand, if only one corner of the forest intersection burns during a fire, there are three other corners available for food and shelter. And if another fire comes through the forest a few years later, destroying one of those three corners, there is still plenty of food and shelter available in the two parts of the neighborhood that are completely unburned. Animals can even revisit the first corner that burned as it regenerates.

But what happens to plants and animals when a fire burns too hot for too long—and hits all corners of the "intersection"? Can *anything* survive?

Fire Fact! Scientists use technology to track patterns in the movements of animals after a fire. They use drones and trail cameras to see which animals are in a specific area, and GPS radio collars and luminescent tags to monitor the movements of individual animals. This information tells scientists where animals have traveled, what resources they most likely went there for, if they visited an area more than once, and how quickly they returned to a burned area.

Fire Fact! Another way scientists study how animals move and behave is by studying their DNA. Samples gathered from hair and blood tell scientists if one group mated with another group from a different area.

# MEGAFIRES

*When fires burn low and slow,* there are benefits: removing old and decaying plant material, recycling nutrients back into the soil, and creating patchworks of habitats. But many of today's fires are burning hotter and spreading faster than ever before.

································· MEGAFIRES ·································

While the exact definition varies among agencies, a **megafire** is generally considered to be a large fire (burning over one hundred thousand acres) that causes an extreme amount of destruction. Megafires spread quickly, burn at hotter temperatures, and are difficult to contain.

Megafires not only threaten the lives of humans, they also wreak havoc on wild animals. Many animals are unable to escape the flames because there's simply nowhere to go. The air is thick with smoke, and the ground becomes so hot that many animals hiding under rocks and stumps are unable to survive. Even streams and ponds may not offer enough protection against the raging flames.

Plants suffer in megafires too. The intense heat from a megafire destroys dormant buds in a tree's bark and raises the temperature of soil so high that underground regenerative tissues are killed.

After some megafires, the destruction is so devastating that the forest never regrows, and animals that were able to escape the flames can't return to their home territory.

Megafires can also lead to mudslides. If too many plants die, there's nothing to hold the soil in place when it rains. Ash, dirt, logs, and snags get swept away by rushing water, burying underground burrows. Some animals become trapped inside their burrows, and the rest must find new places to live.

The devastating effects from a megafire linger for years, touching multiple generations of wildlife. But if fire is a natural occurrence, then why are megafires on the rise? One reason dates back to the Big Burn of 1910.

The "Big Burn of 1910" caused immense damage to acres of land as seen here in the Coeur d'Alene National Forest, Idaho.

········ **THE BIG BURN AND THE U.S. FOREST SERVICE** ········

In the spring of 1910, forests in Idaho, Montana, Washington, and other parts of the United States received little to no rain. The dry ground crunched underfoot. Once fast-flowing rivers slowed to a crawl. By summertime, over one hundred fires were burning. Forest Service rangers and small crews of emergency firefighters were able to keep many of them under control, but violent winds caused the flames to surge. The small fires spread quickly, joining together to form the largest megafire in U.S. history: the "Big Burn."

During the Big Burn, entire trees exploded. Others were ripped from the ground, shooting flames through the air. Firefighters battled the blaze for two days and nights. When rain finally fell on the area, over three million acres of forest had burned. Eighty-seven people died in the fire. Several towns were completely wiped off the map.

Fire Fact! The United States Forest Service was created in 1905 to protect forests and watersheds and to provide the nation with a continuous supply of lumber. Rangers mapped forests, provided access to trails, and protected against poachers and illegal timber harvesting.

Fire Fact! The first forest rangers had to pass both a written and physical test. The written test included questions about ranching and livestock, lumbering, surveying and mapping, forest conditions, and even how to build a cabin. The physical portion included how to saddle and ride a horse, shoot a gun, and walk in a straight line using a compass. Rangers had to provide their own equipment and were paid sixty dollars a month. That's equal to just over two thousand U.S. dollars in 2022.

Fire Fact! The Forest Service often hired local people to help fight forest fires. Many came from mining camps and railroads. Big cities like New York sometimes sent people to help. Unlike rangers, many of these people were untrained and didn't have the appropriate clothing or footwear for working in a forest. Many also spoke different languages, making communicating a challenge.

After the Big Burn, people living in or near forests feared for their safety. Leaders of the Forest Service were also concerned about another megafire. Since they didn't fully understand the benefits of wildfires, they promoted the idea that *all* fires were bad. The Forest Service asked people to put out any fire as soon as possible. They hung up posters that read "One Tree Can Make a Million Matches" and "Stop Woods Fires—Growing Children Need Growing Trees."

Several decades later, the Forest Service decided that their anti-fire campaign needed an official mascot. Smokey Bear appeared on posters and signs throughout national forests, reminding people that "Only You Can Prevent Forest Fires."

Without wildfires, dead trees and debris littered the forest floor. Forests grew more and more dense as smaller trees and shrubs created fuel ladders up to the forest canopy. If and when a wildfire started, it had years of fuel to feed on.

Fire Fact! During the early 1900s, logging was a large industry throughout the United States. Logging companies cut down millions of old, fire-resistant trees and in their place planted species of trees that were less resilient to fire. The combination of letting many forests become overgrown and replacing old-growth forests with groups of young, densely populated trees that can't withstand fire increased the potential for a wildfire to grow out of control.

Fire Fact! By the 1960s, scientific research revealed the positive impact fire can have on the landscape, and in the 1970s the government created policies that allowed fires to burn. But the change came a little too late. The damage to forests had already been done.

## GLOBAL WARMING

Poorly managed, unhealthy forests are only one reason for the increase in megafires. **Climate change** and **global warming** are also to blame.

Climate change describes a change in the average conditions—such as temperature and rainfall—in a region over a long period of time. The United States and many other parts of the world are experiencing warmer, drier, and windier weather conditions.

All it takes is one spark in a hot, dry forest and you have the perfect recipe for a wildfire.

But why is the Earth warming?

For years, people have polluted the Earth by burning **fossil fuels**. Gases emitted from burning fossil fuels are trapped like a blanket in the Earth's **atmosphere**. This blanket also traps the sun's heat, causing the air to become warmer.

Wildfires also contribute to global warming. Smoke from fire pollutes the air, and **carbon dioxide** stored in living plants gets released back into the atmosphere when the plants burn. Pollution and carbon dioxide cause the Earth to become warmer, leading to the possibility of even more megafires.

It becomes a vicious cycle: Warming temperatures cause snow from the mountains to melt earlier in the year. ➜ Early melting leads to a longer dry season and less water for plants to drink. ➜ Without water, plants die. ➜ Dead plants become fuel for wildfires. ➜ Increased air pollution from wildfire smoke. ➜ Warming temperatures. ➜ The cycle continues.

Can we change our behavior and stop the cycle before it's too late?

Pyrocumulus cloud or pyrocumulonimbus over the Mazatzal Wilderness during the Willow Fire near Payson, Arizona

Fire Fact! More and more buildings and homes are built on the edge of forested areas as populations continue to grow. Scientists call these areas Wild Urban Interfaces (WUI). WUIs make it difficult to stop the spread of wildfires because firefighters must divide their time and efforts between saving people and structures and containing the fire. In addition, more wildfires are being started because of the increase in human activity in WUIs.

Fire Fact! Megafires can create their own weather. The intense flames from a megafire rapidly heat the air above the burning forest. As heat rises, it condenses moisture in the air into a cloud. Multiple clouds merge to create a pyrocumulonimbus, or fire-formed, thunderstorm. Pyro-thunderstorms don't produce rain, but they do create wind and lightning, which can lead to even more wildfires.

Fire Fact! The number of megafires each year is increasing around the world due to global warming. In 2019 and 2020, bushfires in Australia burned a record of over forty-five million acres. In the Arctic, which is usually thought to be too wet and cold to burn, wildfires are releasing record amounts of greenhouse gases into the atmosphere.

CHAPTER 8

# FIRE AS A TOOL

## PAST

*Native American tribes across North America* used fire in a variety of ways long before Europeans set foot on the continent. They respected fire, understood its benefits, and saw it as part of their daily lives. In some tribes, fire was used to **fell**—or cut down—trees, shape canoes, and make ceramics. Other Native Americans increased their harvests and improved grazing pastures for their horses by using fire to recycle nutrients back into the soil. Many also used fire to keep nearby fields from growing too tall and forests clear of undergrowth to better spot approaching visitors (who were sometimes friendly—and sometimes not).

Some Native Americans utilized fire as a tool when hunting. Smoke could be waved into hiding holes to flush out prey or wafted into trees so that insects like moths and caterpillars would fall to the ground to be caught and eaten. Often, fires were started to make animals like deer move to a location where they were easier to hunt.

Because tribes had different needs and uses for fire, they started fires at various times of the year and in a variety of locations. As a result, diverse patchworks of habitat formed. Many of the healthy forests used by European settlers were created and maintained by Native Americans.

## PRESENT

In the decades after the Big Burn, most people only thought about the negative impacts of fire. They listened to Smokey Bear and did everything they could to prevent fires from burning. This misunderstanding led to a buildup in fuel, which led to an increase in megafires.

But scientists today are taking what they have learned from Native American burning practices and combining that information with years of new research on forest ecosystems to create ways to better manage forests.

No two forests are the same. What's best for one area may not be the best for another. Knowing how to manage a specific forest requires understanding the needs of the plants and animals that live there.

Before taking action, scientists ask questions like, "Are there plants in the forest, such as lodgepole pine trees, that need fire to reproduce? Has this forest become so overgrown that most wildlife has moved on to look for someplace else to live? Would fire help reset the area? Has this forest been recently burned? Would another fire here help or hurt these animals and plants?"

Because some forests are maintained by government agencies while others are the property of private landowners, these groups must work together, take the answers to these questions into consideration, and then create a management plan.

Management plans often include reducing the amount of burnable material in an area. One way to reduce fuel is to remove it manually. Forest management crews use bulldozers with special attachments or handheld chain saws to cut down smaller trees and shrubs. Removing or thinning these plants not only removes the fuel ladder, it also gives nearby plants a greater share of the available nutrients and more room to grow. Crews remove only trees and shrubs that absolutely need to go in order to maintain the overall health of the forest. They work carefully, trying not to hurt or damage other plants and trees in the area.

Removing fuel by hand is a ton of work! Luckily, there's another quicker way to remove debris from the forest floor—using fire itself.

Fire Fact! Tree rings tell scientists more than how old a tree is. Little black marks on the ring, about the size of a fingernail clipping, show that the tree survived a wildfire. In fire-prone areas, some trees show evidence of surviving more than one fire. Scientists examine rings from a variety of trees in an area to get a complete picture of the forest over time.

Fire Fact! Management plans target sick trees. How do trees get sick? Sometimes bugs get through a tree's bark and damage the inside tissue. Other times bacteria and fungus can attack a tree. While dead trees play an important role in a forest ecosystem, too many dead, sick, or injured trees means there won't be enough healthy trees to support wildlife. Forest managers often remove sick trees to prevent other trees from becoming sick or dying.

## ········· A BURNING PURPOSE ·········

A **prescribed burn**, also called a **controlled burn**, is a fire that is deliberately set and managed by a fire-fighting crew, intended to remove fuel in a given area. There is always a reason for starting a prescribed burn—something forest managers want to achieve through burning. These reasons usually fall into one of three categories.

The first is to remove **activity fuel**. This means fuel that was created by some type of human activity. Maybe a power company cut down a bunch of trees to install a new power line, or a logging company removed a stand of trees. They might have hauled away big logs and left behind smaller branches and debris. If this debris catches fire, it burns hot and is difficult for firefighters to control.

Another reason for starting a prescribed burn is to prevent future fires from reaching homes and buildings. Firefighters create a firebreak around these areas, so that if or when a wildfire starts, these structures have some distance between them and the flames.

The last reason for starting a prescribed burn is to benefit plants and animals. Has your room ever gotten so messy that you can't find what you're looking for? When a forest becomes overgrown, it can be difficult for animals to locate resources. A prescribed burn can act like a "spring cleaning" for the forest floor. Other times, a forest needs to burn so that old plant material is recycled into the soil and dormant seeds have an opportunity to sprout.

With one of these reasons in mind, forest managers work with firefighters to start prescribed burns.

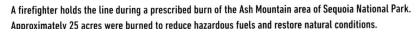
A firefighter holds the line during a prescribed burn of the Ash Mountain area of Sequoia National Park. Approximately 25 acres were burned to reduce hazardous fuels and restore natural conditions.

Firefighters leave a protective ring of vegetation around a duck nest during a prescribed burn.

## BURN PLAN

Prescribed burns are usually planned for the spring and fall, when the weather is cooler and the ground is wetter. Burning at these times of year helps firefighters keep the fire burning low and slow and gives animals a chance to detect and escape the flames.

Before a prescribed burn starts, a team of people works together to create a **burn plan**. The burn boss is responsible for organizing the burn team. Together, the team sets boundaries for the burn based on natural firebreaks, such as rivers and roads. They may also build new firebreaks using shovels and bulldozers. The team looks for potential hazards in the burn area like patches of heavy fuel that could cause the fire to grow larger than desired, as well as sources of water to help put out any unwanted fire.

The burn boss decides how many firefighters are needed on the burn team to safely start and maintain the prescribed burn.

They make sure everyone has the proper equipment to manage the fire and clothing to protect them from the flames. The burn boss also creates a backup plan in case the fire burns differently than expected or jumps a firebreak.

Before the fire is started, the burn boss communicates with people living and working in the surrounding area to let them know that the smoke they'll be seeing and smelling is from a prescribed burn and not from a wildfire. Lastly, they keep an eye on the weather. If it's too dry or windy, the crew must wait until conditions improve.

After reviewing the burn plan checklist, the burn boss tells the crew one of two things:

"No-go. The conditions for burning aren't good. We'll have to wait."

Or, "Let's light it up!"

## GO TIME

Starting a prescribed burn is the job of the ignition crew. From somewhere near the prescribed burn area, a firefighter on the ignition crew switches on a drone. When the firefighter receives the final "go" signal they launch the drone into the sky. Skillfully—and from a safe distance—they guide the drone over the forest canopy and deep into the wilderness, where the trees grow in dense clumps and thick underbrush clutters the forest floor. When they have found their target area, the firefighter clicks a switch. The bottom of the drone opens up and hundreds of fire-starting balls fall from the sky. Within seconds, the balls scatter across the ground. And then, they ignite!

a prescribed fire

s shoot flares from

alk around with **drip**

...ng crew gets to work. The

.. of firefighters who help keep the fire

...y ... ine area designated in the burn plan. This crew

includes a fire effects monitor who roves around collecting information about weather conditions and how a fire is behaving. The fire effects monitor shares this data with the burn boss so that they can adjust the burn plan as needed, and the holding crew prepares to extinguish any unwanted flames.

Fighting fire with fire may seem like an odd approach. But if done for the right reasons and under the right conditions, this process can reduce fuel, keep the forest healthy, and decrease the chance of megafires. However, it requires a lot of time, money, and manpower. That's why some firefighters are looking to animals for help!

Fire Fact! The Plastic Sphere Dispenser (PSD), nicknamed the "ping-pong ball device," is a safer way to start a fire when the location where firefighters want to start the prescribed burn is too difficult to reach by vehicle or foot. Each ping-pong ball contains the chemical potassium permanganate. Just before the balls are dropped, another chemical called glycol is injected into the balls. The two chemicals react, starting a small fire, which quickly feeds on surrounding fuel.

Fire Fact! Fire ecologists are people who study how a fire interacts with its environment. Fire ecologists give firefighters information about how they think the fire will behave, which helps firefighters create a plan for deciding when to let a fire burn and when to try and put it out.

Fire Fact! The topography of the landscape plays a role in how fast and hot a fire burns. Heat naturally rises. Fires that start low in a valley or at the bottom of a hill will spread quickly because the flames have a shorter distance to travel to reach fuel above them. If the fire starts at the top of a hill, it will burn slower because the flames can't reach the fuel below as easily.

# A FIREFIGHTER'S BEST FRIEND

*"Hi. Do you have any goats available?"*

While this question may seem odd, goat herder Lani Malmberg receives this type of call all the time.

Goats are perhaps the most efficient and underutilized fire-fighting tool. Considered nature's munching machines, they can clear acres of overgrown shrubs and weeds in a matter of days. Goats' mouths are made for eating a variety of plants. Their bottom jaw contains eight incisor teeth for biting off leaves and branches and twenty-four molars used for grinding. Goats don't have teeth in their upper jaw. Instead, they have a dental pad that helps rip and tear food.

Goats are built for maneuvering steep, rocky hillsides and dense patches of brush, and their stomachs can digest just about any-thing—poisonous plants, spiky thistle, twigs, trees, vines, cactus, and more. If a goat can reach it, it'll most likely eat it.

Goats prefer to eat plants that grow at eye level or higher. Many even work together by pulling down branches from taller trees and shrubs so that smaller goats can also eat. This ability to eat while standing on their hind legs gives goats an extra leg up. Removing plants that grow seven, eight, or even nine feet off the ground helps reduce the fuel ladder and may prevent fires from reaching the canopy of the tree.

Goat standing on hind legs to reach vegetation

These four-footed weed eaters are particularly helpful in the parts of the United States that go months with little to no rain. The parched landscape fades from lush green to brittle brown and becomes a wildfire risk. Land managers and property owners mow fields and trim back trees and shrubs, but many areas are too steep and rocky for machines to maneuver and too large for people to clear by hand. With each passing rainless day, the landscape becomes drier, creating more fuel. People wonder: Will today be the day flames come for them? Then they make a call.

Lani Malmberg and her goats have been assisting with wildfire pre-vention for over twenty-five years. She travels with her herd from California to Colorado and other areas in the western United States helping public and private landowners reduce **noxious weeds** and decrease wildfire fuel.

The goats hitch a ride to their next meal on a transport trailer, with Lani and her border collie dogs following behind. Once on-site, Lani opens the gate to the trailer. The goats file out and immediately begin eating. Dogs keep members of the herd from wandering too far. If there isn't a creek or river on the property, Lani arranges for a water truck to be delivered and sets up troughs

for the goats. At night, the dogs corral the goats into a fenced-in area where they sleep and digest their food. Large areas of land require Lani's entire herd of twelve hundred goats, while smaller spaces in cities and neighborhoods need only a few hundred.

A goat eating plants in a forest

These firefighting goats do more than just remove plants. They also help restore the health of the soil by fertilizing it with their poop. After all, what goes in must come out! As the goats graze, their hooves massage the poop into the soil. These added nutrients encourage the growth of **native** plant species. It's a win-win, especially for the goats, who get to spend their entire day doing what they love most: eating.

**Fire Fact!** Firefighting goats also play a role in helping to prevent mudslides. Thanks to the goats' fertilizing poop, newly growing plants increase the soil's potential to hold water. When torrential rains fall, the plants and soil stay firmly in place.

Each job comes with risks for both the goats and their herder. Sometimes, goats may be stationed near a wildfire, creating a firebreak to help keep the fire from spreading. Working next to a fire is hot and uncomfortable. The smoky air makes it difficult to breathe.

During one wildfire that Lani and her herd worked, the wind shifted and the fire changed direction. "It was headed straight for us. The goats, dogs, and I ran down the hill alongside bears, mountain lions, and other animals fleeing the flames." Unfortunately, some of Lani's goats did not survive.

Wild animals also pose a risk to the herd. Every now and then, a bear or mountain lion kills a goat. Lani accepts this as part of the job and understands that wild animals need to eat too. More often than not, though, it's humans and their pets, such as unleashed dogs, who pester and harm her goats.

Luckily, people are learning about the benefits of using goats to prevent wildfires. Some farmers and ranchers keep a small herd to manage the land around their property. Others are venturing into the goat–land management business after receiving training from people like Lani and through nonprofit organizations such as Goatapelli.

For Lani, it's about asking, "How do we value the land? How can we respectfully live and work on it to ensure health and vitality for the animals that also call the land home, for generations to come?"

While goats are a great option for people living in fire-prone areas, there's another four-footed animal joining in the fight against wildfires.

# BEAVER BRIGADE

*Each day, the beaver brigade inspects its toolkit:*

- **Long, sharp teeth? Check!**
- **Waterproof coat? Check!**
- **Powerful feet and tail? Check!**

These beavers may not call themselves firefighters, but they do help to slow the spread of wildfires—one tree at a time.

A beaver dam at Grand Teton National Park, Wyoming

Beavers use their strong jaws to fell trees and **dam** waterways. After a dam is built, beavers scoop up muck and mud from the bottom and sides of the waterway and use it as cement to hold the dam together. Unable to pass through the beaver's dam, the water flow slows and pools, eventually creating a pond.

Whew, that's a lot of work! And it doesn't stop there.

In this pond, beavers build a home, also called a **lodge**. Beavers need hundreds of trees to build their dam and even more to build their lodge. So what happens when their tree supply runs low? They look nearby for more trees.

Beavers are master swimmers, but clumsy and vulnerable to predators on land. To get the additional logs and branches they need, they create new waterways. Beavers use their strong front paws to dig canals further into the surrounding forest. Then they use the canal to float felled trees back to the lodge and dam.

These canals help water spread like a spider's web, farther and farther away from the dam. This abundance of water **saturates** the ground surrounding the beaver's dam. Plants growing in the area have plenty of water, even during a drought. If a wildfire spreads through the area, that stored-up water makes plants more resistant to burning and slows the spread of the fire.

A beaver family that stays in an area for a long time might permanently transform the landscape into wetland. (When the ground remains consistently saturated, the area changes from forest to wetland.) Wetlands help contain a fire since wet wood is less likely to burn. Wetlands and ponds also provide refuge for animals fleeing from a fire. As for the beavers, they hunker down inside their lodges and wait for the fire to pass.

Fire Fact! Beavers can sense the speed and movements of water currents. This helps them choose the best place to build a dam.

Fire Fact! The simplest way for a beaver to make a dam is to add sticks and branches to a log or large tree trunk that lies across and touches both sides of the stream bank. If a suitable log isn't available, beavers will stick smaller logs and branches into the muddy river bottom like a row of fence posts, then weave more branches in and around the posts. If that's not possible, the beaver leans logs and branches against one another in a pile until the pile stretches across the streambank.

Fire Fact! Beavers can fell a tree in a matter of minutes, depending on the size and variety of tree. The beaver stands on its hind legs, using its powerful tail for support, like a kickstand on a bike. Next, the beaver uses its sharp nails to tear bark off. After the bark has been removed, the beaver circles the tree, biting and chewing through chunks of wood until the tree crashes to the ground!

## THE ULTIMATE PURIFICATION SYSTEM

Even after the flames go out, a beaver's dam plays an important role in helping the area to recover. As the wind dies down, ash and debris from burning plants land in waterways. Ash in the water is like smoke in the air—it chokes the water, making it difficult for animals below the surface to breathe. The situation gets worse for **aquatic animals** if it rains soon after a fire. Without plants to hold the soil in place, more debris washes into the waterway. This new deposit of pollutants can be deadly.

Animals living upstream from the dam may feel the effects of wildfire-polluted water for a long time. Downstream, wildlife thrives as if the fire never happened. Why? Because of the beavers' brilliant filtration system.

Water flows quickly down a waterway without a dam. This faster rate of flow causes ash and debris in the water to be constantly churned up. When the water reaches a beaver dam, its flow slows way down. This allows the ash and debris to settle to the bottom of the pond. The water in the pond clears up, and aquatic animals can breathe more easily once again.

Beaver dams help stop the spread of fire and aid with vegetation regrowth postfire.

Humans also benefit from this filtration system. Clean water means they can return to fishing and swimming in the waterway soon after the fire has gone out.

Given all that beavers do to fight fires and restore the landscape, you might hope for a thriving beaver population. At one point, there was! Scientists believe there were as many as two hundred million beavers engineering ecosystems across North America prior to the 1700s. But as European settlers moved West, they hunted beavers for their fur. By the end of the 1800s, the beaver population plunged so low that they nearly went **extinct**.

After years of conservation efforts and reintroducing beavers into their native habitats, beaver populations have bounced back. Scientists estimate as many as fifteen million beavers currently live in North America.

Despite their firefighting services, many people consider beavers pests because their dams can cause roads and neighborhoods to flood. And with the threat of megafires increasing, scientists can't stand by and wait for people to change their minds about these creatures. Instead, they have invented ways to simulate a beaver's engineering skills in fire-prone areas.

**Post-assisted log structures (PALS)** are made up of untreated wood posts and other natural materials that mimic the buildup of woody plants in the bottom of a waterway. A **Beaver Dam Analog (BDA)** is a man-made structure designed to mimic the form and function of a natural beaver dam.

Both types of structures are cheap and easy to construct, and they serve the same purpose—to simulate a beaver's ability to slow down, saturate, and filter water. They range in size and shape depending on the area. However, PALS and BDAs are temporary structures. They are no replacement for beavers themselves. To really make a dent in decreasing megafires, it takes a collective—beavers, goats, forest managers, and even you—working together to improve the health of forests.

 Fire Fact! BDAs are sometimes built before relocating or releasing a beaver back into the wild. BDAs create a deep pool of water for beavers to swim in. This deeper water provides protection from predators. A BDA also saves beavers time and energy because they can use the structure and make it stronger instead of having to build something from scratch.

# FIRE, THE FUTURE, AND YOU

*The relationship between fire and nature is complex,* interwoven, and ever-changing. A tiny spark grows into a massive fire. A massive fire transforms a living tree into a snag. Some things die, allowing other things to live. Everything that happens in nature creates a ripple effect of additional events and changes—including some that are good and others that are not.

There's still so much to learn about our natural world, and *you* can be part of the team that discovers the answers.

Students study forest regeneration at a national park in Alaska.

Maybe someday you'll research the behavior of animals or help to create wetlands and restore beaver populations. Maybe you'll become a fire ecologist and study fires around the world.

Maybe you'll find yourself jumping out of a plane to fight fires in remote landscapes. Maybe you'll be the proud owner of a herd of firefighting goats. Or maybe you'll be a veterinarian, helping injured animals recover so they can be released back into the wild.

No matter your interests, we can all work together to understand how our actions affect the world around us, to do our part to fight climate change, and to build a better planet.

# FOLLOW THAT FLAME!

A group of wildland firefighters head out during the 2010 Rainbow Bridge Fire, North Cascades National Park, Washington.

*Help wanted: Must have above-average physical and mental strength and be able to tolerate extreme heat, thick smoke, and insect bites. Must be a team player and able to work twenty-four-hour shifts for two weeks at a time in remote locations. Picky eaters need not apply.*

After the Big Burn of 1910, detecting, locating, and extinguishing wildfires became a priority for people living in or near forested areas. The Forest Service built fire lookout towers on mountain ridges high above the treetops across the country. Each tower was staffed by a lookout, whose job was to scan the forest for smoke and report the location of the fires to local firefighting crews.

Many lookout towers are still in service today, though most have been updated with more high-tech detection strategies. Cameras provide a live 360-degree video feed of the forest twenty-four hours a day, seven days a week. Firefighters at fire stations monitor these feeds and call a dispatcher when they spot smoke.

The dispatcher answers the emergency call. After gathering information about a fire, the dispatcher initiates a firefighting response by contacting a duty officer. Every piece of land in the United States is marked as a **zone** on a map. The dispatcher knows which duty officer to call based on the fire's zone location.

Each zone has a set of automatic instructions to deploy. These instructions are called **run cards**. The number and kind of resources listed on the run card is determined by the zone's size and location. Zones may have multiple run cards for different size and intensity fires.

The duty officer looks at the run card for that zone and then activates the appropriate firefighting crews.

Each year thousands of firefighters risk their lives to fight wildfires head on. While the basic principles of firefighting remain the same whether fighting a fire in the middle of a city or in a remote forest (safely contain and extinguish the fire), a fire in the wilderness takes additional knowledge and skills.

Firefighters get evaluated based on their physical abilities and technical knowledge to make sure they are qualified for the job. They must know how to use and care for their equipment, have a strong understanding of how fire behaves, know the effects wildfires have on the landscape, and demonstrate the proper techniques for starting and extinguishing fires.

These skilled workers continually train and build on their experience in order to build **competency**. Some training can be completed online. Other training is done in person, where firefighters practice using their equipment and learned skills to fight small, controlled fires. In-person training also gives firefighters an opportunity to practice working together as a team and helps them to understand the role their team plays when fighting fire.

**Wildland firefighters** work seasonally from late spring to early fall. When they get a call that a fire has started, wildland forest firefighters grab their gear and link up with their crew at the base camp.

Before heading out to their work site, the incident commander, or person overseeing the firefighting operation, tells firefighters about the weather conditions, estimated fuel type, and topography of the landscape to better predict how the fire will behave. Firefighters also need to know where current firebreaks exist, the best places to build more, any nearby sources of water, and escape routes to be used in case the fire gets out of control.

Fire Fact! A person must be at least eighteen years old to apply to be a wildland firefighter. Firefighters take a Work Capacity Test (WCT) to prove they are capable of performing the minimum firefighting duties. The most challenging category of the test—arduous pack test—requires a firefighter to complete a three-mile walk over level terrain in forty-five minutes or less while carrying a forty-five–pound pack.

Fire Fact! Wildfires can start at any time of day or night. Firefighters must always be ready to stop what they're doing and join their crew. In many wildfire locations, there's no reception to call home to let their loved ones know they're okay. Firefighters depend on the person fighting next to them, as well as other crews in the area, to work together to keep everyone safe.

Fire Fact! A base camp is set up in a safe anchor point, or location close to the fire that can't burn. The safe anchor point may be a stretch of roadway, land near a lake or stream, or on a rock outcropping. At the base camp, firefighters wake early for breakfast, then head out with their crew. After a long day on the front line, firefighters return to camp to eat dinner, clean their gear, and get a few hours of sleep before waking up to do it all over again in the morning. Some crews may work far away from base camp and sleep outside overnight.

Fire Fact! Many firefighters carry a meal-ready-to-eat (MRE) in their pack or grab a brown-paper-bag lunch before leaving base camp. For really large, long-burning fires, a restaurant or catering company may be brought out to feed firefighters at the base camp.

Fighting a massive blaze requires multiple crews, each with specialized jobs.

Ground crews are first to respond to and attack a fire. Ground crews are made up of hand crews, engine crews, or both. Hand crews primarily use shovels, rakes, or a special wildfire firefighting tool called a Pulaski to create firebreaks. Hand crews sometimes use chain saws to remove small trees and brush and drip torches to set **backfires**.

Backfires are similar to prescribed burns but on a much smaller scale. They are intentionally started in front of a wildfire—when the wildfire reaches the backfire, it will run out of fuel and no longer be able to spread.

Hand crews often hike miles to their work site. There, they split up into teams, or squads. One person from each squad is named the squad leader. The squad leader is responsible for overseeing the safety of the group, directing the firefighting efforts, and communicating with people back at base camp.

An engine crew may work alongside a hand crew or as an independent team. They use hoses to spray water from a fire truck to wet the ground ahead of the fire or spray water directly on the base of the flames.

Heavy machinery operators help the ground crews by bulldozing a clearing or felling large trees to create a firebreak. The primary goal of ground crews is to keep the fire contained by preventing it from crossing the firebreak.

Sometimes a wildfire starts in a place so remote that the teams can't drive or hike to it. Anyone up for a quick flight? **Helitack** crews catch a ride to their work site on a helicopter. The aircraft lands near the fire and offloads the crew. If landing isn't possible, the helitack crew **rappels** from the helicopter as it hovers just

Wildland firefighters rappel to a landing zone in the Perreau Creek, Idaho area as part of their annual training.

above the forest. Once on the ground, the helitack crew uses chain saws and hand tools to create firebreaks. If the crew rappels down, they'll also clear an area for the helicopter to land so that it is able to safely pick them up.

**Hotshots** are highly skilled groun⌐
hottest and most dangerous p⌐
work for long periods of ⌐
carry an additional ten
are often flown into t⌐
tools, including additi
chain oil. Firefighters m⌐
and be able to pass tougher ⌐

**Smokejumpers** make up a sm⌐
parachute from planes into a fire. Befor⌐
leaves the plane, the pilot circles the area above the ⌐⌐⌐⌐⌐
The team assesses the situation, determines how many people are needed to fight the fire, and chooses the best place for them to land.

After they land, the smokejumpers gather their gear and create a small base camp. Smokejumpers carry some supplies with them, including a knife to cut themselves free if their parachute gets stuck in a tree on the way down. Other supplies get dropped to them by plane, such as hand tools, food, water, and camping equipment. For the next forty-eight hours, smokejumpers work without the help of any other crews, creating firebreaks and fighting the flames.

Pilots do more than transport helitack and smokejumper crews to their work sites. They also help fight fires! Pilots may wet the ground by dropping water from buckets that hang from the underside of the aircraft, or drop fire-retardant chemicals ahead of the fire to try to stop it from spreading. Pilots can also radio ground crews, letting them know where a fire is under control and where it continues to spread.

Since some conditions are too dangerous for firefighters, they need another tool to help detect, monitor, and fight fires. **Drones** are a type of **unmanned aerial vehicle (UAV)**. They are smaller than traditional aircraft and easy to maneuver. Drones also have the

Black Mountain Hotshots hiking into the northwest side of the 2020 Slink Fire in the Humboldt-Toiyabe National Forest in California

ability to fly in conditions that are unsafe for piloted aircraft, such as at night or in thick smoke. Drones can start prescribed burns and take **thermal images** of fire. These images show firefighters exactly where the fire is burning and how far it has spread.

Fire Fact! The first smokejumper unit was formed in the 1940s, when the Forest Service experimented with better ways to respond to and fight fires. Today, there are nine smokejumper bases located across Idaho, Montana, California, Oregon, Washington, and Alaska. The bases are strategically located to be able to respond to wildfires as quickly as possible. Smokejumpers may also travel to other parts of the United States and the world.

Fire Fact! Parachuting into a forest is risky business. Smokejumpers wear jumpsuits made of Kevlar to protect them from becoming injured as they crash through trees and shrubs. Special padding inside the suit softens their landing.

Fire Fact! Pilots are required to take a basic firefighting course to ensure they can understand and use common phrases when communicating with firefighters on the ground. Pilots also receive certifications which designate their ability to transport people or do a water-bucket or fire-retardant drop.

Fire Fact! Only firefighters who are actively fighting a wildfire have permission to fly a drone over a wildfire area. Unauthorized drones can cause accidents for firefighting pilots.

All firefighters wear special clothing to keep them safe during fires. Fireproof pants and jackets and leather boots and gloves protect firefighters from the heat, helmets protect their heads from falling debris, and goggles keep heat off their faces and smoke and ash out of their eyes. In addition to hand tools, firefighters carry two-way radios, food, water, first aid kits, and **fire shelters**.

Fire Fact! A firefighter's pack can weigh as much as sixty pounds.

Fire Fact! The Pulaski is a tool unique to wildland firefighters. The head of the Pulaski is attached to a handle usually made of wood, fiberglass, or plastic. On one end of the head is an axe used to chop wood. On the other end of the head, an adze is used to dig up soil. The combination of two tools in one allows a firefighter one less piece of equipment to carry. The Pulaski was invented by Ed Pulaski, a forest ranger, while fighting the Big Burn of 1910.

Fire Fact! Fire shelters are used by firefighters as a last resort if they become trapped and can't escape the flames. Made from aluminum foil woven with silica, the shelter can withstand heat up to 2,000° F for up to one minute. It takes about twenty-five seconds for a firefighter to pull the fire shelter out of their pack, shake it open, and wrap it over their body. Firefighters must lay as low to the ground as possible, digging a small depression into the dirt for their nose and mouth in order to breathe. Firefighters are trained to plan and look for an escape route and to use a fire shelter only as a last resort.

As more wildfires occur, people continue to shift the way we view and respond to fires. We no longer believe that all wildfires need to be extinguished. Our new understanding is that sometimes allowing fires to burn is beneficial.

When choosing whether to fight a fire or let it burn, firefighters take a few things into consideration. First, they look at which zone a fire is in. Are there people and buildings nearby that need defending, or is the fire in a remote area where no one will get hurt? They ask, "What are the risks of this fire continuing?"

Firefighters also consider the time and resources needed to contain a fire. Sending multiple crews to battle flames that will eventually put themselves out because of natural firebreaks is a waste of time and money.

Crews construct a fire break around the Spruce Canyon Fire, Washington.

They also let fires burn if it's what's best for the landscape, especially if the area contains fire-dependent plants.

Some wildfires burn for only a few hours. Others may burn for days or weeks. Really large fires may burn for months.

Even after a fire has been extinguished, firefighters have lots of work to do. This period is called the mop-up stage. During the mop-up stage, firefighters revisit burned areas in search of hotspots—areas that could reignite. They flip over smoldering logs and shovel dirt or pour water on areas that are still warm to the touch.

When the mop-up stage is finished, firefighters return to base camp to clean and inspect their gear, and replace anything that is damaged. A call from the dispatcher could come in a week, in a month—or even the next day.

A civilian tanker releases fire retardant over the
Government Flats Complex Fire in Oregon.

# ACKNOWLEDGMENTS

*In December 2017*, I walked out of a store to discover gray-white flakes drifting down from the sky. It took me a few seconds to realize the flakes weren't snow. They were ash.

The wildfire was still far enough away that we didn't need to worry—yet. But only a few miles away, the stable where my daughters took riding lessons was already in the process of evacuating their horses. It was a very scary period for everyone in the area.

A few years later, we hiked through a previously burned forest. I noticed that while blackened tree trunks still showed evidence that a fire had happened, the rest of the forest was green and alive with life. I began to wonder, is all wildfire bad? What does wildlife do as fire rages through its home? And what happens in the forest after the flames die out? I thought, if I had questions about wildfires, maybe others did too.

A huge heartfelt thanks to my editor, Sally Morgridge, for giving me the opportunity to share what I discovered about wildfires with others. Your enthusiasm, creativity, and keen editorial eye helped make this book the best that it could be. Thank you to the rest of the team at Holiday House for working so hard behind the scenes.

To Kate, Natasha, Nora, Jacqueline, Mary, and others who provided various feedback along the way, thank you for sharing your time and talents with me. The kidlit community is the absolute best.

Thank you to Gavin Jones, Sallysue Stein, Lani Malmberg, Shawn Borgen, and Patrick Antone for contributing to the content and accuracy of this book. And to wildland firefighters who risk their life each time they fight a blaze.

Lastly, to my husband and daughters, thank you for encouraging me to follow my dreams, for pretending to listen as I drone on about more wildfire facts and the writing process, and for allowing me the time and space needed to get the words out. There's no other team I'd rather be a part of.

ACTIVITY FUEL: fuel that was created by some type of human activity

ADAPT: to adjust oneself to different conditions

ADZE: a tool similar to an axe, with an arched blade at right angles to the handle, used for cutting large pieces of wood

AMPHIBIAN: a cold-blooded animal that has a backbone and smooth skin with no scales. Amphibians spend part of their lives in water (breathing with gills) and part of their lives on land (breathing with lungs).

AQUATIC: growing, living in, or frequenting water

ATMOSPHERE: the whole mass of air surrounding the Earth

BACKFIRE: an intentionally started fire used to slow or stop the advance of an existing fire

BEAVER DAM ANALOG (BDA): a man-made structure designed to mimic the form and function of a natural beaver dam

BIRD: a warm-blooded animal that has a backbone, feathers, wings, and a beak

BURN PLAN: an operational plan for managing a specific fire to achieve resource benefits and management objectives

BUSHFIRE: an Australian term used to describe an uncontrolled fire in a bush area

CAMBIUM TISSUE: a thin formative layer between the xylem and phloem of most vascular plants that gives rise to new cells and is responsible for secondary growth

CANOPY: the uppermost spreading branches of a forest

CARBON DIOXIDE: a colorless, odorless gas that is formed by animal respiration and in the decay or combustion of animal and vegetable matter and is absorbed from the air by plants in photosynthesis

CARBON MONOXIDE: a colorless, odorless gas that is formed as a product of the incomplete combustion of carbon or a carbon compound

COUNTY ANIMAL RESPONSE TEAMS (CARTS): groups of individuals who work together to aid in animal evacuations during wildfire emergencies

CLADOPTOSIS: an annual dropping of twigs or branches

CLIMATE CHANGE: long-term changes in temperature and weather patterns

COLLAGEN: a structural protein

found in skin and other connective tissues

COMPETENCY: having sufficient knowledge, judgment, skill, or strength in regard to a certain area

CONTROLLED BURN: a fire that is deliberately set and managed

CROWN FIRE: a fire that burns at the top, or crown, of a tree, often well in advance of the fire on the ground

DAM: a barrier preventing the flow of water

DECIDUOUS TREE: a tree whose leaves fall off or shed and that becomes dormant during the winter

DEHYDRATE: to lose water or bodily fluids

DERMIS: a layer of skin or tissue lying below the epidermis

DORMANT: not actively growing

DRIP TORCH: a handheld device for igniting fires by dripping flaming liquid fuel on materials to be burned

DRONE: an uncrewed aircraft guided by remote control or onboard computers

ECOSYSTEM: a community of organisms and their environment functioning as an ecological unit

EMACIATED: abnormal thinness caused by a lack of nutrition or illness

EPIDERMIS: the outer layer of skin of a vertebrate that overlies the dermis

EUTHANIZE: the act of permitting the death of hopelessly sick or injured individuals

EXTINCT: no longer existing

EXTINGUISH: to cause to cease burning

FELL: to cut, knock, or bring down

FIREBREAK: a barrier of cleared land that helps stop the spread of fire

FIRE ECOLOGIST: a person who studies how a fire interacts with its environment

FIRE REGIME: a pattern of fire occurrence including time, frequency, and intensity

FIRE-RETARDANT CHEMICAL: a chemical that has the ability or tendency to slow or halt the spread of fire

FIRE SHELTER: a portable safety device used by wildland firefighters as a last resort when trapped by wildfire

FOSSIL FUEL: fuel—such as coal, oil, or natural gas—formed in the earth from plant or animal remains

FUEL: organic matter, either living or dead, that is available to burn

FUEL LADDER: living or dead vegetation that allows a fire to climb from the forest floor into the tree canopy

GAUZE: loosely woven surgical dressing made from cotton

GENERATOR: a machine by which mechanical energy is changed into electrical energy

GERMINATE: to begin to grow; to sprout

GLOBAL WARMING: an increase in the Earth's atmospheric and oceanic temperatures

GPS RADIO COLLAR: a collar with an attached radio transmitter used to remotely track the movement of an animal

GROUND FIRE: a fire that consumes organic material beneath the surface

HARDY: capable of withstanding adverse conditions

HELITACK: a team of firefighters that are transported to a wildfire by helicopter

HOTSHOT: a highly trained, skilled, and experienced wildland firefighter that works near the hottest part of a wildfire

HOT SPOT: a location that has a higher temperature than surrounding areas

HYDRATE: having absorbed enough water or liquid

IMMOBILIZE: to reduce or eliminate motion; to fix in place

IMPING: to graft into a wing

INDICATOR SPECIES: an organism that indicates the health of an ecological community

INSTINCTS: natural or innate impulses, inclinations, or tendencies

INTRAVENOUS (IV): within a vein

JACOBSON'S ORGAN: a scent organ consisting of a pair of sacs or tubes typically in the roof of the mouth in many vertebrates, notably snakes and lizards

LODGE: a beaver home

LUMINESCENT TAG: a tag that glows or emits light

MAMMAL: a warm-blooded animal that has a backbone and grows hair at some point during its life

MEGAFIRE: a fire that burns over a large area of land

MOLT: to periodically shed hair, feathers, shell, or horns

NATIVE: living or growing naturally in a particular region

NOXIOUS WEED: a plant that is physically harmful or destructive to living beings

NUTRIENT RECYCLING: the way in which elements are continuously broken down and/or exchanged for reuse between living and non-living components in nature

OLFACTORY CUES: chemical signals received by the olfactory system that represent incoming signals typically received through the nose

ORGANIC: without use of chemically formulated

fertilizers, growth stimulants, antibiotics, or pesticides

OVIPOSITOR: specialized organ through which female insects deposit eggs

POST-ASSISTED LOG STRUCTURE (PALS): a man-made structure that promotes the process of wood accumulation in a waterway

PATCHWORK: something made up of a variety of pieces or parts

PEAT: an organic material found in marshy or damp regions composed of partially decayed plant matter

PERSISTENT SEED: a seed that remains viable (alive) in the soil for more than one season

PIONEER: a person, group, or thing that is the first to develop a new method or activity

PIONEER TREE: a tree that is among the first to colonize an area that has been altered through a physical or natural occurrence

PLASTIC SPHERE DISPENSER (PSD): a device used in prescribed or wildland fire applications to remotely ignite fuel

PRESCRIBED BURN: a fire that is deliberately set and managed by a firefighting crew, intended to remove fuel in a given area

PREY: an animal that is caught and killed by another for food

PULASKI: a wildland firefighting tool invented by forest ranger Ed Pulaski during the Big Burn of 1910

PYROPHILIC SEED: a seed that needs fire to germinate

PYROPHYTE: a plant that has adapted in a way that makes it resistant to fire

PYROCUMULONIMBUS STORM: a thunderstorm that forms during and as a result of a megafire

RAPPEL: to descend by sliding down a rope

RED FLAG WARNING: an alert to the public of conditions that may lead to the rapid spread of a hazardous natural condition

REPTILE: a cold-blooded animal that has a backbone and skin covered with small, hard plates called scales

RESPROUTING: the growth of new plant material from dormant buds

RUN CARD: instructions regarding which resources to deploy during a wildfire

SANITIZE: to reduce or eliminate pathogens, such as bacteria, on the surface of something

SATURATED: unable to absorb further moisture

SECONDARY CAVITY NESTERS: animals that rely on abandoned cavities created by primary cavity nesters

SEDATE: to administer a drug to create a relaxed physical state

SEED BANK: the supply of seeds present in a given area

SEROTINOUS CONE: a cone covered in resin that must be melted for the cone to open and seeds to be released

SHELTERING IN PLACE: seeking safety in an area one already occupies

SIMULATE: to give or assume the appearance or effect of something

SMOKEJUMPER: a wildland firefighter that parachutes into to a hard-to-reach location in order to fight a wildfire

SNAG: a dead tree that is left upright to decompose naturally

SUCCESSION: the regrowth of a forest that happens over hundreds of years

SURFACE FIRE: a fire that burns on the surface of the ground, consuming fuel such as grass, leaves, twigs, and shrubs

THERMAL IMAGE: an image formulated by infrared radiation and thermal energy

TOPOGRAPHY: the arrangement of the natural and artificial physical features of an area, often delineated on a map

TORPOR: a state of lowered physiological activity typically characterized by reduced metabolism, heart rate, respiration, and body temperature

TRAIL CAMERA: an outdoor camera used to take unattended photographs or video footage

TRANQUILIZE: to administer drugs to make an individual calm

TRANSIENT SEED: a seed that remains viable (alive) in the soil for less than one season

UNMANNED AERIAL VEHICLE (UAV): an aircraft that is remotely operated without any human pilot, crew, or passengers on board

VETERINARIAN EMERGENCY RESPONSE TEAM (VERT): a group of emergency responders who quickly and efficiently mobilize resources needed to help animals affected by wildfire and other natural disasters

WILDLAND FIREFIGHTER: a person whose job is to suppress wildfires on land that has not been cultivated by human activity

WILDLIFE DISASTER NETWORK (WDN): an American organization focusing on aiding wild animals suffering due to natural disasters

WILD URBAN INTERFACE (WUI): buildings and homes built on or near the edge of forested areas

ZONE: a section of an area set off as distinct from surrounding or adjoining parts, or an area created for a particular purpose

**CHAPTER 1**

*"Fire acts like a living organism"*: "Here's What It's Like to Be Inside the California Wildfire," Environment, National Geographic, July 30, 2018, https://www.nationalgeographic.com/environment/article/news -wildfire-california-photography.

*"issues red flag warnings . . . to the rapid spread of wildfires"*: Brian Donegan, "8 Facts You Might Not Know about Large Wildfires and Weather," The Weather Channel, June 16, 2020, https://weather.com/safety/wildfires /news/2020-06-16-facts-you-may-not-know-about-large-wildfires-and -weather.

*"warm temperatures, low humidity, and strong winds"*: "Red Flag Warning," National Weather Service, accessed October 4, 2022, https://www .weather.gov/mqt/redflagtips.

**CHAPTER 2**

*"giraffes are too tall to fit under freeway overpasses"*: Patrick Antone, phone interview with author, April 6, 2022.

**CHAPTER 3**

*"Without the ability to climb and hunt for food, the foxes' chance of survival was low"*: Sallysue Stein, phone interview with author, April 22, 2022.

*"low-lying tree branches, shrubs, and smaller trees found under the canopy of a larger tree"*: "Ladder Fuels," Surviving Wildfire, August 27, 2019, https: //surviving-wildfire.extension.org/ladder-fuels/.

*"Their skins are usually discarded"*: Amy Quinton, "Healing Burned Animals with Fish Skins," UC Davis, September 17, 2018, https://www.ucdavis.edu /health/news/healing-animals-with-fish-skins.

*"found in most kinds of wood . . . orange or dark yellow"*: Kevin Beck. "What Are the Colors of a Fire & How Hot Are They?" Sciencing, February 24, 2020, https://sciencing.com/colors-fire-hot-8631323.html.

CHAPTER 4

*"ovipositor deep into the wood"*: Ken Gibson, "Management Guide for Horntails (Wood Wasp)," USDA Forest Service, July 2010, https://www.fs.usda.gov /Internet/FSE_DOCMENTS/stelprdb5187453.pdf.

*"Black-backed woodpeckers are sometimes used as an indicator species"*: "Black-Backed Woodpeckers & the Emerging Threat of Homogenous Forest Fires," American Ornithological Society, August 6, 2019, https: //americanornithology.org/black-backed-woodpeckers-the-emerging -threat-of-homogenous-for-est-fires/.

*"Researchers from the U.S. Forest Service Pacific Southwest Research Station (PSW)"*: Stephanie Worley Firley, "In Recently Burned Forests, a Woodpecker's Work Is Never Done," U.S. Department of Agriculture, February 21, 2017, https://www.usda.gov/media/blog/2015/06/18 /recently-burned-forests-wood-peckers-work-never-done.

*"A tree's outer layer of bark acts as a shield"*: "Anatomy of a Tree," arborday .org, accessed September 13, 2022, https://www.arborday.org/trees /ringstreeanatomy.cfm.

*"Snags are dead trees . . . it becomes a log"*: "Trees and Snags—Garden for Wildlife," National Wildlife Federation, accessed September 13, 2022, https: //www.nwf.org/Garden-for-Wildlife/Cover/Trees-and-Snags.

CHAPTER 5

*"The seed bank is the supply of seeds present in a given area,"*: "Home | US Forest Service," accessed September 13, 2022, https://www.fs.usda.gov/rm /pubs/rmrs_gtr042_2.pdf.

## CHAPTER 7

*"releasing record amounts of greenhouse gases"*: Ed Struzik, "The Age of Megafires: The World Hits a Climate Tipping Point," Yale Environment 360, Yale School of the Environment, September 17, 2020, https://e360.yale.edu /features/the-age-of-megafires-the-world-hits-a-climate-tipping-point.

*"One Tree Can Make a Million Matches"*: Stephen J. Pyne, *Fire in America* (Seattle, WA: Univ. of Washington Press, 1997).

*"Stop Woods Fires—Growing Children Need Growing Trees"*: Pyne.

*"Climate change describes a change in the average conditions—such as temperature and rainfall—in a region over a long period of time"*: "What Is Climate Change?" Climate Kids, NASA, 2022, https: //climatekids.nasa.gov/clmate-change-meaning/.

## CHAPTER 9

*"the wind shifted and the fire changed direction"*: Lani Malmberg, phone interview, April 28, 2022.

*"wild animals need to eat too"*: Malmberg.

## CHAPTER 10

*"as many as two hundred million beavers engineering ecosystems"*: Isobel Whitcomb, "Beaver Dams Help Wildfire-Ravaged Ecosystems Recover Long after Flames Subside," Scientific American, February 7, 2022, https://www .scientificamerican.com/article/beaver-dams-help-wildfire-ravaged -eco-systems-recover-long-after-flames-subside/.

*"A Beaver Dam Analog (BDA) is a man-made structure designed to mimic the form and function of a natural beaver dam"*: "Beaver Dam Analogs," Anabranch Solutions, accessed September 19, 2022, https: //www.anabranchsolutions.com/beaver-dam-analogs.html.

## BONUS CHAPTER

*"carry more robust tools,"*: Shawn Borgen, phone interview, October 4, 2022.

ABC News. "'Like a Freight Train': Firefighters Describe What It's Like Riding out a Wildfire in a Fire Shelter, Their Last Resort for Safety." ABC News. Last modified October 6, 2020. https://abcnews.go.com/US/freight -train-firefighters-describe-riding-blaze-fire-shelter/story?id=73420186.

"About Us." Goatapelli Foundation. Last modified August 10, 2022. https: //goatapellifoundation.org/about-us/.

"Aircraft." National Interagency Fire Center. Accessed September 23, 2022. https://www.nifc.gov/resources/aircraft.

Alaska Department of Fish and Wildlife. "Succession—Changing Forest Habitats." *Alaska's Forests and Wildlife*, 2001. https://www.adfg.alaska.gov /static-sf/statewide/aquatic_ed/AWC%20ACTIVITIES/FORESTS%20&%20 WILDLIFE/BACKGROUND%20INFORMATION/Forests%20IV_Succe ssion%20Facts.pdf.

American Museum of Natural History. "Fire Chaser Beetles Sense Heat from Miles Away." American Museum of Natural History. December 22, 2017. https://www.amnh.org/explore/news-blogs/news-posts/fire-chaser -beetles-sense-heat-from-miles-away.

"Anatomy of a Tree at Arborday.org." Arbor Day Foundation. Accessed September 23, 2022. https://www.arborday.org/trees/ringstreenatomy.cfm.

Anguiano, Dani. "Burned Paws, Hungry Bears: The Race to Help Animals Injured in Wildfires." *Guardian*. August 22, 2021. https://www.theguardian .com/environment/2021/aug/22/california-wildfire-animal-rescue.

Ballenger, Joe. "Los Angeles Is Burning: So What's Happening to the Bugs?" Ask an Entomologist. September 15, 2018. https://askentomologists .com/2018/01/02/los-angeles-is-burning-so-whats-happening-to-the -bugs/.

"Beaver Dam Analogs." Anabranch Solutions. Accessed September 23, 2022. https://www.anabranchsolutions.com/beaver-dam-analogs.html.

Beck, Kevin. "What Are the Colors of a Fire & How Hot Are They?" Sciencing. February 24, 2020. https://sciencing.com/colors-fire-hot-8631323.html.

Bell, Ryan. "What Happens When Livestock Are in the Path of a Wildfire." *National Geographic*. September 4, 2015. https://www.nationalgeographic .com/culture/article/what-happens-when-livestock-are-in-the-path-of-a -wildfire.

"Birthday of the U.S. Forest Service: February 1, 1905." National Wildfire Coordinating Group. Last modified October 2021. https://www.nwcg.gov /committee/6mfs/usfs-birthday.

Brown, James K.,and Jane Kapler Smith, eds. *Wildland fire in ecosystems: effects of fire on flora*. General Technical Report 42, vol. 2 (Dec. 2000). U.S. Department of Agriculture, Forest Service, Rocky Mountain Research Station. https://www.fs.usda.gov/rm/pubs/rmrs_gtr042_2.pdf.

Canon, Gabrielle. "How a Tahoe Refuge Saved Owls, Coyotes and Raccoons from Wildfire." *Guardian*. September 5, 2021. https://www.theguardian. com/us-news/2021/sep/05/caldor-fire-animal-refuge-rescue-evacuation.

Cornell Lab. "All About Birds—Black-backed Woodpecker." Accessed September 23, 2022. https://www.allaboutbirds.org/guide/Black-backed _Woodpecker/overview.

Cornell, Maraya. "How Zoos Protect-and Evacuate-Animals during Wildfires." *National Geographic*. November 17, 2018. https://www.nationalgeographic .com/animals/article/zoos-protect-animals-fire-disaster.

Cotton, S., and T. McBride. "Caring for Livestock during Disaster—Fact Sheet No. 1.815." Colorado State University. https://extension.colostate.edu/docs /pubs/livestk/01815.pdf.

DeBano, Leonard F. "The Effect of Fire on Soil Properties." SoLo. USDA Forest Service Rocky Mountain Research Station. https://forest.moscowfsl.wsu .edu/smp/solo/documents/GTRs/INT_280/DeBano_INT-280.php.

Donegan, Brian. "8 Facts You Might Not Know about Large Wildfires and Weather: The Weather Channel." Weather Channel. June 16, 2020. https://weather.com/safety/wildfires/news/2020-06-16-facts-you-may-not-know-about-large-wildfires-and-weather.

Ecological Society of America. "Fire Ecology." Ecological Society of America. Last modified 2002. https://www.esa.org/esa/wp-content/uploads/2012/12/fireecology.pdf.

"Fire Mitigation." Living Systems. Accessed October 4, 2022. https://www.livingsystemslandmanagement.com/fire_mitigation.html.

Forest History Society. "Fire Lookouts." Forest History Society. Accessed September 23, 2022. https://foresthistory.org/research-explore/us-forest-service-history/policy-and-law/fire-u-s-forest-service/fire-lookouts/.

Frontline Wildfire Defense. "Forest after Fire—Restoration & Regrowth after Wildfire." Frontline Wildfire Defense. May 25, 2022. https://www.frontlinewildfire.com/wildfire-news-and-resources/how-forest-recovers-wildfire/.

Geluso, Kenneth N., and Thomas B. Bragg. "Fire-Avoidance Behavior of Meadow Voles (Microtus Pennsylvanicus)." *The American Midland Naturalist* 116, no. 1 (1986): 202–5. https://doi.org/10.2307/2425953.

Gibbons, Gail. *Beavers.* New York: Holiday House, 2014.

Gleason, Karen Miranda, and Shawn Gillette. "Myth Busting About Wildlife and Fire: Are Animals Getting Burned?" *Fire Management Today* 69, no. 1 (winter 2009): 26–28. https://www.fs.usda.gov/sites/default/files/fire-management-today/69-1.pdf.

"Goat Grazing for Fire Mitigation." Goat Green. Accessed October 4, 2022. https://goatseatweeds.com/goat-grazing-for-fire-mitigation/.

Goldfarb, Ben. "How Beavers Became North America's Best Firefighter." *National Geographic*. Last modified September 23, 2020. https://www .nationalgeographic.com/animals/article/beavers-firefighters-wild -fires-california-oregon.

Gottesman, Kyra. "Wildlife Network Works to Heal Animals Injured by Wildfires." *Enterprise-Record* (Chico, CA). October 16, 2020. https: //www.chicoer.com/2020/10/16/wildlife-network-works-to-heal -animals-injured-by-wildfires/.

Grafe, T. Ulmar, Stefanie Döbler, and K. Eduard Linsenmair. "Frogs Flee from the Sound of Fire." *Proceedings: Biological Sciences* 269, no. 1495 (2002): 999–1003. http://www.jstor.org/stable/3068180.

Hadley, Debbie. "How Do Insects Smell?" ThoughtCo. March 10, 2019. https: //www.thoughtco.com/how-insects-smell-1968161.

Helvarg, David. "Fireball-dropping Drones and the New Technology Helping Fight Fires." *National Geographic*. October 16, 2020. https: //www.nationalgeographic.com/science/article/fireball-dropping-drones -new-technology-helping-fight-fires.

"How Does Fire Kill Trees?" USDA Forest Service. https://experience.arcgis. com/experience/5a66ef88db6a49e29e77cabc6d7c3cdc/page/Background/.

Joosse, Tess. "Veterinarians Form New Network to Heal Wildlife Animals Burned in Wildfire." *Mercury News*. December 28, 2020. https: //www.mercurynews.com/2020/12/28/veterinarians-form-new -network-to-heal-wildlife-animals-burned-in-wildfire/.

Joyce, Christopher. "How the Smokey Bear Effect Led to Raging Wildfires." NPR. August 23, 2012. https://www.npr.org/2012/08/23/159373691/how -the-smokey-bear-effect-led-to-raging-wildfires.

Keeley, Jon E., and C. J. Fotheringham. "Smoke-Induced Seed Germination in California Chaparral." Ecological Society of America. Last modified 1998. https://www.uv.es/jgpausas/teach/3469-Keeley1998Ecology79.pdf.

Kelsey, Rodd. *Wildfires and Forest Resilience: the case for ecological forestry in the Sierra Nevada.* Unpublished report of the Nature Conservancy (Sacramento, CA: 2019).

Kerlin, Katherine E. "Wildlife Disaster Network Mobilizes Aid for Burned, Injured Wildlife." UC Davis. October 5, 2020. https://www.ucdavis.edu /climate/news/wildlife-disaster-network-mobilizes-aid-for-burned -injured-wildlife.

Kiester, Jr., Edwin. "Using Goats to Prevent Wildfires." *Smithsonian Magazine.* Last modified October 2021. https://www.smithsonianmag.com /science-nature/using-goats-to-prevent-wildfires-51327045/.

"Ladder Fuels." Surviving Wildfire. August 27, 2019. https://surviving-wildfire .extension.org/ladder-fuels/.

Lazarus, Sarah. "Goats Are the Latest Weapons in the War Against Wildfire." CNN. Last modified April 9, 2019. https://www.cnn.com/2019/04/08 /americas/goats-and-wildfires-intl/index.html.

Levitan, Dave. "How Drones Could Help Fight Wildfires Supercharged by Climate Change." Grid News. Last modified April 13, 2022. https: //www.grid.news/story/climate/2022/04/13/how-drones-could-help -fight-wildfires-supercharged-by-climate-change/.

Lima-Junior, Edmar Maciel, Manoel Odorico de Moraes Filho, Bruno Almeida Costa, Francisco Vagnaldo Fechine, Maria Elisabete de Moraes, Francisco Raimundo Silva-Junior, Maria Flaviane Soares, Marina Becker Rocha, and Cybele Maria Leontsinis. "Innovative Treatment Using Tilapia Skin as a Xenograft for Partial Thickness Burns after a Gunpowder Explosion." *Journal of Surgical Case Reports* 2019, no. 6 (2019). https://doi.org/10.1093/jscr/rjz181.

Linley, Grant D., Chris J. Jolly, Tim S. Doherty, William L. Geary, Dolors Armenteras, Claire M. Belcher, Rebecca Bilege Bird, et al. "What Do You Mean, 'Megafire'?." *Global Ecology and Biogeography* 31, 10 (Oct. 2022) . https://doi.org/10.1111/geb.13499.

Llamas, Andreu. *Secrets of the Animal World: Beavers: Dam Builders.* 1996.

"Management Guide for Horntails (Wood Wasp)." US Forest Service. Accessed September 23, 2022. https://www.fs.usda.gov/Internet/FSE_DOCUMENTS /stelprdb5187453.pdf.

Manata, Megan. "California Cities Turn To Hired Hooves To Help Prevent Massive Wildfires." NPR. Last modified January 5, 2020. https: //www.npr.org/2020/01/05/792458505/california-cities-turn-to -hired-hooves-to-help-prevent-massive-wildfires.

McGlashen, Andy. "An Introduction to Imping, the Ancient Art of Feather-Mending." Audubon. December 22, 2017. https://www.audubon.org /news/an-introduction-imping-ancient-art-feather-mending

"Meet the Crew—Prescribed Fire Personnel." Deschutes Collaborative Forest Project. Last modified April 30, 2019. https://deschutescollaborativeforest .org/forest-restoration/meet-the-firefighters/.

Moskal, Emily. "After a Wildfire, Fire-Chasing Beetles Swarm in to Lay Their Eggs." *Bay Nature.* January 8, 2014. https://baynature.org/article/fire -chasing-beetles-make-appearance/.

Mullen, Luba. "How Trees Survive and Thrive after a Fire." National Forest Foundation. Summer/Fall 2017. https://www.nationalforests.org/our -forests/your-national-forests-magazine/how-trees-survive-and-thrive- after-a-fire.

Nag, Oishimaya Sen. "What Are the Adaptations of Pyrophytes or Fire-Resistant Plants?" WorldAtlas. September 13, 2019. https://www.worldatlas.com /articles/what-are-the-adaptations-of-pyrophytes-or-fire-resistant-plants. html.

National Fire Fighter Wildland Corporation. "Top Tools & Tactics for Conducting Prescribed Fires." National Fire Fighter Corp. Last modified August 11, 2017. https://www.nationalfirefighter.com/blog/Top-Tools -Tactics-for-Conducting-Prescribed-Fires#.

National Geographic. "Here's What It's Like To Be Inside the California Wildfire." *National Geographic.* Last modified July 31, 2018. https: //www.nationalgeographic.com/environment/article/news–wildfire –california–photography.

National Interagency Fire Center. "Crews." National Interagency Fire Center. Accessed September 23, 2022. https://www.nifc.gov/resources/firefighters /crews.

Nimmo, Dale. "Animal Response to a Bushfire Is Astounding. These Are the Tricks They Use to Survive." The Conversation. January 7, 2022. https: //theconversation.com/animal-response-to-a-bushfire-is-astounding –these-are-the-tricks-they-use-to-survive-129327.

Nimmo, Dale, Alexandra Carthey, Chris Jolly, and Daniel T. Blumstein. "Welcome to the Pyrocene: Animal Survival in the Age of Megafire." *Global Change Biology.* August 17, 2021. https://doi.org/10.32942/osf.io/46zgd.

Nimmo, Dale G., Sarah Avitabile, Sam C. Banks, Rebecca Bliege Bird, Kate Callister, Michael F. Clarke, Chris R. Dickman, et al. *Animal movements in fire-prone landscapes,* n.d. https://doi.org/10.1111/brv.12486.

"Noxious Weed Management." Goat Green. Accessed October 4, 2022. https: //goatseatweeds.com/noxious–weed–management/.

"Our History." US Forest Service. Last modified May 17, 2022. https: //www.fs.usda.gov/learn/our–history.

"Overhead." National Interagency Fire Center. Accessed September 23, 2022. https://www.nifc.gov/resources/firefighters/overhead.

Parker, Laura. "How Megafires Are Remaking American Forests." *National Geographic.* Last modified August 9, 2015. https: //www.nationalgeographic.com/science/article/150809–wildfires –forest-fires-climate-change-science.

Parker, V. Thomas. "Soil seed bank." Encyclopedia Britannica. March 31, 2021. https://www.britannica.com/science/soil-seed-bank.

Petruzzello, M. "Playing with Wildfire: 5 Amazing Adaptations of Pyrophytic Plants." Encyclopedia Britannica. April 7, 2014. https://www.britannica.com/list/5-amazing-adaptations-of-pyrophytic-plants.

Powell, Hugh. "Old Flames: The Tangled History of Forest Fires, Wildlife, and People." All About Birds. 2019. https://www.allaboutbirds.org/news/old-flames-the-tangled-history-of-forest-fires-wildlife-and-people/.

Pyne, Stephen J. *Fire in America: A Cultural History of Wildland and Rural Fire.* University of Washington Press, 1997.

Quinton, Amy. "Healing Burned Animals with Fish Skins." UC Davis. September 17, 2018. https://www.ucdavis.edu/health/news/healing-animals-with-fish-skins.

Scott, Aaron. "Could 'Smokey Beaver' Help Fight Wildfires?" Oregon Public Broadcasting. Last modified November 13, 2021. https://www.opb.org/article/2021/11/13/oregon-beaver-conservation-wildlife-science-environment/.

Shahverdian, Scott, Joseph M. Wheaton, Stephen N. Bennett, Nick Bouwes, Reid Camp, Chris Jordan, Elijah Wayne Portugal, and Nick Weber. "Mimicking and Promoting Wood Accumulation and Beaver Dam Activity with Post-Assisted Log Structures and Beaver Dam Analogues." In *Low-Tech Process-Based Restoration of Riverscapes: Design Manual,* edited by Joseph M. Wheaton, Stephen N. Bennett, Nick Bouwes, Jeremy D. Maestas, and Scott Shahverdian. Logan, UT: Utah State University Restoration Consortium, 2019. https://doi.org/10.13140/RG.2.2.22526.64324.

Sherriff, Lucy. "Wombats: The Furry Heroes of the Australian Wildfires." Discovery. Last modified May 26, 2020. https://www.discovery.com/nature/wombats--the-furry-heroes-of-the-australian-wildfires.

Skropanic, Jessica. "'We've Learned How Resilient Nature Is': Animals Recovering from California Fires Get a Little Help." *USA Today.* October 3, 2021. https://www.usatoday.com/story/news/nation/2021/10/03/california-fires-vets-wildlife-rescues-work-save-animals-fires/5982343001/.

Smith, Jane Kapler. "Wildland Fire in Ecosystems: Effects of Fire on Fauna." *USDA Forest Service Rocky Mountain Research Station*. January 2000. https://doi.org/10.2737/rmrs-gtr-42-v1.

"Smokey the Beaver: Beaver-Dammed Riparian Corridors Stay Green During Wildfire Throughout the Western United States." Ecological Society of America. Last modified September 2, 2020. https://doi.org/10.1002/eap.2225.

Solly, Meilan. "How the Los Angeles Zoo Prepares Its Animals to Face Natural Disasters." *Smithsonian Magazine*. November 14, 2018. https://www.smithsonianmag.com/smart-news/los-angeles-zoo-prepares-animals-natural-disasters-180970773/.

Stillman, Andrew. "Black-Backed Woodpeckers & the Emerging Threat of Homogenous Forest Fires." American Ornithological Society. August 6, 2019. https://americanornithology.org/black-backed-woodpeckers-the-emerging-threat-of-homogenous-forest-fires/.

Struzik, Ed. "Fire-Induced Storms: A New Danger from the Rise in Wildfires." *Yale Environment 360*, Yale School of the Environment. Last modified January 24, 2019. https://e360.yale.edu/features/fire-induced-storms-a-new-danger-from-the-rise-in-wildfires.

"The Age of Megafires: The World Hits a Climate Tipping Point." *Yale Environment 360*. Yale School of the Environment. Last modified September 17, 2020. https://e360.yale.edu/features/the-age-of-megafires-the-world-hits-a-climate-tipping-point.

"The Unconventional Weapon Against Future Wildfires: Goats." *New York Times*, September 18, 2021. https://www.nytimes.com/2021/09/18/business/wildfires-goats-prevention.html.

Tidwell, Tom. "Thinking Like a Mountain, About Fire." US Forest Service. Last modified May 22, 2010. https://www.fs.usda.gov/speeches/thinking-mountain-about-fire.

"Trees and Snags—Garden for Wildlife." National Wildlife Federation. Accessed September 13, 2022. https://www.nwf.org/Garden-for-Wildlife/Cover/Trees-and-Snags.

U.S. Fire Administration. "Wildfire and the Wildland Urban Interface (WUI)." U.S. Fire Administration. Accessed September 23, 2022. https://www.usfa .fema.gov/wui/.

"U.S. Forest Service Fire Suppression." Forest History Society. Accessed September 23, 2022. https://foresthistory.org/research-explore/us -forest-service-history/policy-and-law/fire-u-s-forest-service/u-s -forest-service-fire-suppression/.

Vartan, Starre. "How Does Wildfire Smoke Affect Wildlife? Here's What We Know." *National Geographic*. October 19, 2021. https: //www.nationalgeographic.com/animals/article/how-does-wildfire -smoke-affect-wildlife.

Vermont Barn Fire Prevention Task Force. "Evacuation of Livestock During a Fire." Accessed September 23, 2022. https://ocgov.net/sites/default/files /E911/Agriculture%20Emergencies/Evacuation%20of%20Livestock%20 During%20a%20Fire%208-30-10%20Final.pdf.

"What Is Climate Change?" Climate Kids. NASA. Last modified September 8, 2022. https://climatekids.nasa.gov/climate-change-meaning/.

"What Causes Wildfires? Understanding Key Risk Factors." Frontline Wildfire Defense. Last modified May 11, 2022. https://www.frontlinewildfire.com /wildfire-news-and-resources/what-causes-wildfires/.

Whitcomb, Isobel. "Beaver Dams Help Wildfire-Ravaged Ecosystems Recover Long After Flames Subside." *Scientific American*. Last modified February 7, 2022. https://www.scientificamerican.com/article/beaver-dams-help -wildfire-ravaged-ecosystems-recover-long-after-flames-subside/.

"Wildland Fire." US Forest Service. Accessed September 23, 2022. https: //www.fs.usda.gov/managing-land/fire.

"Wildland Fire: What is a Prescribed Fire?" National Park Service. Last modified March 19, 2020. https://www.nps.gov/articles/what-is-a- prescribed-fire.htm.

"Wildland Fire in Ecosystems Effects of Fire on Fauna." US Forest Service. Accessed September 23, 2022. https://www.fs.usda.gov/rm/pubs/rmrs_gtr042_1.pdf.

Williams, Gerald W. "The USDA Forest Service—The First Century." US Forest Service. Last modified April 2005. https://www.fs.usda.gov/sites/default /files/media/2015/06/The_USDA_Forest_Service_TheFirstCentury.pdf.

Woelfle, Alice. "Animal Evacuation during a Wildfire: How to Plan and Where to Go." KQED. September 30, 2020. https://www.kqed.org/news/11840375 /animal-evacuation-during-a-wildfire-how-to-plan-and-where-to-go.

Worley Firley, Stephanie. "In Recently Burned Forests, a Woodpecker's Work Is Never Done." U.S. Department of Agriculture. February 21, 2017. https: //www.usda.gov/media/blog/2015/06/18/recently-burned-forests-wood -peckers-work-never-done.

Yong, Ed. "Fire-Chasing Beetles Sense Infrared Radiation from Fires Hundreds of Kilometres Away." *Discover Magazine.* May 28, 2012. https: //www.discovermagazine.com/planet-earth/fire-chasing-beetles-sense -infrared-radiation-from-fires-hundreds-of-kilometres-away.

Zug, George R. "Jacobson's Organ." Encyclopedia Britannica. April 12, 2018. https://www.britannica.com/science/Jacobsons-organ.

## INTERVIEWS

Antone, Patrick. Phone Interview. April 6, 2022. Chapter two.
Stein, Sallysue. Phone Interview. April 22, 2022. Chapter three.
Malmberg, Lani. Phone Interview. April 28, 2022. Chapter nine.
Borgen, Shawn. Phone Interview. October 4, 2022. Bonus chapter.

Bill McMillan, Wikimedia Commons: 32

Bitterroot National Forest: iv, v, 3

Brad Werwinski: 12

Bruce Fields, U.S. National Park Service: 41

Cavan Images: 46

Charity Parks, United States Department of Agriculture: 87, 91

Dan Ng, U.S. National Park Service: 63

Eric Neitzel, Wikimedia Commons: 54

Gold Country Wildlife Rescue: 25, 27, 28

I.C.E. Products USA: 13

Jerry McBride, *Durango Herald*: iii, 7

Jessica Stremer: 35

John Moeykens, U.S. National Park Service: 61

Joseph Wheaton, Utah State University, Creative Commons: 76

Karin Higgins, University of California: 26

Kyle Miller, Wyoming Hotshots, USFS: i, vi, 1, 88–89

Lance Cheung, United States Department of Agriculture: 86

Library of Congress Prints & Photographs Division: 50

Neal Herbert, Department of the Interior: 39

North Cascades National Park Service Complex, U.S. National Park Service: 81

Oren Peles, Pikiwiki Israel: 67

Robert Hynes, U.S. National Park Service: 34

Scott Bauer, U.S. Department of Agriculture: 69

Spc. Matthew Burnett, 115th Mobile Public Affairs Detachment: 92–93

U.S. Forest Service: 2

U.S. National Park Service: 56, 60, 72, 79

University of Minnesota: 29

Washington Department of Natural Resources, Northeast Region: 90

https://www.fws.gov/program/fire-management
https://www.fs.usda.gov/managing-land/fire
https://www.nifc.gov/
https://www.doi.gov/wildlandfire/joint-fire-science-program